Endorsement by Sheriff Joe Arpaio

I've dedicated my life to Law Enforcement, serving my community, our Constitution and this great nation.

Police Officers make up some of the finest men and women and the responsibility of serving as one is reserved for those with the greatest integrity and who understand honor, pride and respect.

Dominick Izzo writes about the internal fortitude required to serve as well as maintaining your drive and passion as you continue to serve throughout your years as a cop.

I have been following Izzo for years and have watched as his own struggles, sacrifices and police service shaped him into the voice and leader that law enforcement needs as we move forward together.

Before the Badge is a must read if you are testing to become a cop, are a cop or support our cops and should be carried by all police academies nationwide.

Joe Arpaio
Maricopa County Sheriff

BEFORE THE BADGE

by
Dominick Izzo

© 2019 by Dominick Izzo. All rights reserved.
Words Matter Publishing
P.O. Box 531
Salem, Il 62881
www.wordsmatterpublishing.com

No part of this publication may be reproduced, stored in a retrieval system, or transmitted in any way by any means—electronic, mechanical, photocopy, recording, or otherwise—without the prior permission of the copyright holder, except as provided by USA copyright law.

ISBN 13: 978-1-949809-46-6

Library of Congress Catalog Card Number: 2019953618

TABLE OF CONTENTS

Chapter One - I Won't Back Down 1

Chapter Two - They Couldn't Handle The Truth 9

Chapter Three - The Man In The Mirror…What Changed Me 13

Chapter Four - Why Do You Want To Be A Cop? 21

Chapter Five - Fearless And Unapologetic 33

Chapter Six - Don't Become A Cop—Just Don't…Unless 43

Chapter Seven - The Academy 53

Chapter Eight - My First Night On Patrol 61

Chapter Nine - A Good Cop But Only Human 71

Chapter Ten - The Power Of God 81

Chapter Eleven - A Nazi, The Devil And
"What The Hell Is Going On?" 95

Chapter Twelve - Tears And Guilt 101

Chapter Thirteen - You Give Cops A Bad Name 109

Chapter Fourteen - Race And Sex 119

Chapter Fifteen - The Great Pretender 129

Chapter Sixteen - The Good Fight—Restoring The Badge 141

Chapter Seventeen - Ever Changing Times and Your Place In It .. 161

Appendix I 167

Appendix II 195

Chapter One

I WON'T BACK DOWN

MY OPEN LETTER TO ALL COPS:
Look, if you're a cop, retired or have any vested emotional interest in law enforcement, you come to any of my platforms and feel the need to remind me of my status in law enforcement, let me go ahead and save you some time.

See, the thing is, unlike most cops, retired cops, ex-cops and whatnot, I will be the first to admit that police officers are a bunch of insecure, self-righteous, pissed off men and women who think they have more power than has actually been given to them. And I was one of the worst of them all.

However, between those who have wives and husbands nagging on you at home, the shit bags you deal with on the street, the media breathing down your neck and your command staff looking to bend you over and drive it in raw for one misspelled word in a report, cops are a bunch of disillusioned pawns who actually think that their name will outshine their badge numbers. The damn sad truth that none of them really see is how easily replaceable they are with anyone who's willing to say two words: "Yes, sir."

Loved one day, hated by command the next. You've all seen it.

Am I salty, pissed off, disgruntled for what happened to me? Absolutely. I texted some pics of some dead bodies to an idiot who worked for me and was a holster sniffer and wanted to be a cop more than anything. I wanted to share with him what I did for a career and "relate" in some way. Bad choice on my end.

Do I regret sending the photos? Nope. I have done it my whole career. As my then FTO in 2001 (who's now deputy chief) told me, "Go out and get a disposable camera, so you can show your family and friends what you deal with." Hell, even the idiot who fired me has a whole phone, laptop and desktop filled with the most gruesome pictures you have seen which he would make sure he showed you when you were next to him, so he could tell you all about what he did on those cases.

But my decision got me in hot water and the man who was never a cop and just landed the job as chief of police because of his political pull, had it out for me because I was suing him for watching me piss in the bathrooms on camera. Is what it is. That's what retaliation lawsuits are for, and I refuse to settle or back down.

Some asshat, who never did a day of work in this job, dictated my career and I made the decision to fight, not resign, have my jacket sealed and move to another department. Some took the easy way out and did resign. I said, "Fuck it. Fire me."

Some of you out there know exactly what it is like to have that target on your back. And rest assured, the rest of you will know what it's like at one point in your career. Happens to the absolute best of them.

"Izzo, you couldn't make it as a cop!"

Thank God. Here's what "making it as a cop" looks like:

Being fifty years old and not being able to retire yet because you need insurance for you (and you're family if you have one) and having to stick around for another five years, at least while you find a part-time job you can stomach IF your department approves it.

Making it in law enforcement is working at the same place for twenty plus years, bitching about the exact same crap, watching new guys come in who think they know it all, all while watching kiss-asses get promoted to command which you'll just complain about later that you should have gotten that rank, but you didn't take the test, and you look like an idiot for complaining.

Making it in law enforcement means coming to work every day wondering when command picks you as a target since their annual rotation of discipline is coming your way, and you know it. Then you act completely shocked at how you could have done so much for a department to treat you with such disrespect; all the while it hits you that you stood by in complete silence for years and watched it happen to others.

Making it in law enforcement means that you have a nagging wife who bitches about your schedule and why you have to work on the holidays again this year, and you go to work pissed off, knowing that you'll come home and won't get any for a month now. Hell, you start to wonder if she's stepping out behind your back because those little holster-sniffing badge bunnies that like you are starting to look good too.

Making it in law enforcement means being a female cop who scares off every man she dates because she's so used to being the power top on the street with every man she pulls over, and wonders why every guy gets sick of her bullshit after twenty years on the job and not knowing how to interact with people on a human level.

Making it in law enforcement means twenty years of building an identity that only comes to life when you put on your superhero costume. Keeping your mouth shut because some guy who's got a gold star to your silver star can make your life a living hell, so you take it out on those you interact with in the street.

And that's when your inner self finally feels worth, and the world gets to see you as you stand out with the word "police" printed on you. I mean, how else would they know who you are?

Making it in law enforcement means finally pulling the plug, having nowhere to go every day at roll call, seeing that the pension you busted your ass over for two decades is only enough if you live in a one-bedroom apartment and eat oodles of noodles and get basic cable.

Making it in law enforcement is the exact same as ending your high school football years.... It was glorious at the time and you were elevated to "god" status by your fans, but rivaled by your own teammates. And in the end, when you're off the field and not even a coach or official, no one remembers you, you forgot all other aspects of your life and you find yourself at the local 7-11 as you walk past the new generation of cops and you find yourself saying, "I remember when…"

I loved being a cop, more than most anything. But it makes me feel sad for those who think the end of a journey isn't really the end of their identity.

Keep telling me I couldn't "make it as a cop."

The joke is on you. I kept my identity. Yours is still a series of numbers on your chest that will be taken away from you and belong to someone else one day.

Serving the public isn't the same as being a slave. But you'll figure it out.

See, unlike you order takers who lost yourselves somewhere around year five, right where the ideals of what you swore an oath to and that paycheck with massive security meet, you loved the concept of what you did all while bitching about it every single day. You know how I know this? Because I was surrounded by it and did it too.

But, I am not like most of you. No wife, no kids and a massive chip on my shoulder to prove a right and fight a wrong.

I loved the idea of what being a cop meant. Truth, the law, brotherhood, community, value. The very best of ourselves.

I challenged a mayor in one village, a chief in another and then decided this last time that no one was going to take what I earned this last time.

But cops are cops and eat each other alive when their insecurities kick in, and I have seen the truth behind that "brotherhood" and how easily that blue wall crumbles.

I have turned my back on others who needed it all because

of the "blue group think" and absolute fear of department retaliation. And I regret every single time I didn't fight.

So, when social media took us all by storm, and I was fortunate enough to have a voice, I used it. And trust me, it cost me more than you know.

The truth is, you can't stand for anything different than what you hope to be. Again, I was there. I felt that too.

In the animal kingdom, geese won't associate with other geese who have been mutilated or disfigured. That goose is shunned and dies. Happens with cops too. You have no clue the abandonment you will potentially face as an outcast by your brethren, should your time under the command staff microscope come.

"Izzo, you're a disgrace and got fired!"

Yep. Texted a picture of a man on all fours in the closet of his house, fully clothed and dead. Texted another picture of an eighty-six-year-old woman who suffocated in a pool of her own blood after having a ruptured upper GI.

I still have a picture album somewhere with car crashes, stabbings, a guy with his nose blown open and blood and snot all over, drunks passed out in ditches covered in vomit, a shooting or two and a bunch of great pictures of families, kids, events and more.

The disgraced side of me comes from the fact that I actually thought that the men and women I was fighting for in my department would stand with me when it came time to take the drastic move of fighting back.

But you see, that's where I was the fool. They had wives, kids, pensions, mortgages, car payments, all things that I didn't have to worry about. They ran out of fear faster than I would run to a free cheeseburger day at McDonald's.

And in the end, the blue brotherhood is self-serving to those who are scared shitless of the only power they have ever known being taken away from them. And that power comes at a great personal cost. You lose who you are, and your identity becomes "Officer."

The only thing more powerful than a man or woman with the lawful authority to rip a person out of their home or car just because they can articulate it in a report is the man or woman who can take away that authority just because they have a personality conflict with them.

Gang, I was a full-time cop and sworn in, in March of 2001, I have done it all, just like you, having worked in a town where the clientele consisted of the shit that Chicago and Milwaukee chased out as well as the most amazing men and women who truly understood the meaning of the word "community."

I have seen the horror, cried on my drive home, hated every single aspect of mankind, used my badge to get women and cheat on my girlfriends, lied to myself about who I was and lost it all just to find myself again.

Cops eat other cops. I have seen it all too often in the face of saving one's own ass.

So, when you come here and misspell your comments (I have no idea how some of you get your reports approved) and think that reminding me of my own trail of shit even compares to you… you are absolutely right. You do not compare to me at all.

I have spent far too long defending myself from a position that, sadly, one day you might face. And the countless men and women who contact me with their horror stories of department betrayal would scare the living shit out of you.

See, I got fired. I may go back, who knows as that's up to lawyers, judges and God.

But until then, and even after then, you can hate me all you want for my mouth. You can call me a disgrace, an embarrassment, or whoever you need me to be to satisfy the anger you have for what you're stuck in.

But I will still fight for you because you represent all that is good in what we all loved doing. You are the warriors that we need. You are those that I look up to and hold my hopes highest for your success. Because without you, our way of life is chaos.

But, I will remind you, as you turn those corners in your

squad, write those tickets, take those bullshit calls for service… you are still a slave to a system that can get rid of you any damn time they find a reason to.

And all I want to do is make it so that the world sees your value.

I am arrogant. I am overcome with pride. I am absolutely self-righteous and own every single aspect of it.

Hate me all you want. I am the only one who's out here saying exactly what you can't so long as you wear that badge.

And the moment I stop is the moment where I give up on all that I believe in you. I pray that never happens.

Be safe, go home to your families, and kindly, from the bottom of my heart, go fuck yourself if you have a problem with me.

After all, we are family and family fights.

- Izzo

Chapter Two

THEY COULDN'T HANDLE THE TRUTH

"Resign, or they will fire you." Those were the words of my Union rep after my three-hour interrogation for texting the pictures of the man who died from the overdose and the woman who died from a ruptured upper GI. Not to mention the other garbage they tried to trip me up on.

He told me that they were pissed that I didn't lie. And that's what you need to know right off the bat. If you are a cop and your command staff asks you questions, make the absolute assumption that they already have the answers, and are judging to see how you answer them. It is always a trap of integrity testing.

My integrity is unshakable, so I wasn't ever worried.

See, the thing about any police interrogation, be it on a citizen or one of their own, is that they already have the answers before they ask any question, it's good police work. So, during my interrogation, I simply told the truth. Over and over and over again, and it pissed them off hardcore.

I don't lie, I just don't. And I felt both the frustration of the village attorney's face when he didn't get me to slip up, change my answers, or flat out lie. And I felt the seething look of contempt from my chief as he also knew that I wouldn't give him the easy way out and get his way to be able to discredit me, my service as a cop or my name.

My union rep told me that the chief and village attorney offered me a Loudermill Hearing. It's a hearing where I basically get to plead my case to the two men who want to fire me, on why I shouldn't be fired. It's for them to watch you grovel in front of them. Pure ego bullshit.

"They can go fuck themselves and fire me," was my answer back.

So, I was fired. I accepted it, and as of this book, I am still fighting it. I was brought up on 56 charges for department policy violations ranging from Facebook posts in uniform to texting photographs of dead bodies. Yes, I did it, and I do not apologize. I was a cop, and cops have a certain way of being cops.

As of the time this book is finished, I am in a lawsuit with my department for retaliation against me after I demanded my chief's resignation for his involvement in our department's body cameras recording us in the bathroom, his role in the Melissa Calusinski case, the Fox Lake Police Officer suicide of Charles G.I. Joe Gliniewicz and later the case of Marni Yang and her involvement in the death of a pregnant girlfriend of a former Chicago Bear.

On December 19th, 2016, I was stripped of my police title, authority, powers, credentials and life as a cop.

Nearly three years later and after running in the election for Cook County (Chicago) Sheriff, giving police integrity speeches across the nation, becoming the host of a national radio show and finding life after law enforcement, I would do it all again just to take on the fights that need to be fought.

And in the end, it was nothing more than social media that opened the door to expose the police corruption that had always gone unnoticed, unchecked and protected and left my audience in complete disbelief; yet for once, full of hope that there are some cops out there who still believe in the badge. And believe me when I say this, there are thousands of men and women who wear that badge who silently stand watch and are exactly who you need them to be.

Chapter Three

THE MAN IN THE MIRROR... WHAT CHANGED ME

Politics didn't change me. Neither did social media fame. Age, experience and Brian all changed me.

Brian was a grown man in bod but had not aged past sixteen years. I knew his older brother briefly, his mother until the time of her death and his sister to this day.

Brian's mother was sick, his older brother was his primary caretaker, and his sister worked several jobs to help the family out financially.

They had all been residents of the town I worked in, far long before I was an officer there. Every cop who came before me knew of Brian and all the new officers who came after me had their exposure to him as well.

Our town was very small and very simple. It was also not very affluent with the average household income of less than fifty thousand dollars per year.

Most homes were crammed with several people sharing rooms; sometimes six or more in a two-bedroom house with shared beds and makeshift sleeping arrangements in the other rooms, etc.

In the summer, you'd see people walking the street at all

hours of the night. Not too many homes had air conditioning, and not too many people had jobs. So when the night hours came, people would walk outside to get out, clear their minds or find the peace they couldn't find in a house shared with so many others.

Brian was one of those who walked at night…EVERY NIGHT.

Summer or winter, during my years there, I saw Brian either walking or riding his bicycle in the dark. And he was intoxicated every single time.

Brian worked in the town doing odd jobs for people. He mowed lawns, cleaned up properties, etc. He lived, worked, and played in the immediate square mile that he lived in. People would pay him cash, and he would drink it by day's end.

By day's end, Brian's personality was also the lunar opposite to his sunny disposition which preceded it.

During the day, Brian was quiet. He was meek. He barely spoke and was very polite and a complete boyish gentle soul….

But at night, after he had drunk his pay, he was one of the most verbally combative men I had ever met.

"Fuck you! Get your quota!" He would say that on every single contact we made with him.

He was loud too. We would get noise complaint calls and find Brian walking down the middle of the road and yelling out loud to himself.

But, in spite of all that verbal yelling and threatening talk, he was as harmless as anyone ever could be.

I was told by some of the older officers, that in the past, they had arrested Brian numerous times for public intoxication. But after the umpteenth time, the judge had advised that not only could Brian not comprehend what he was doing, but he was not able to pay for the citations.

Later, it was discussed, that in Illinois, public intoxication is not an enforceable law and is prohibited by the state, so officers stopped arresting him for it.

So, for all my time working in Brian's town, every single officer knew what the standard procedure was when they got a call or saw Brian. It was to do their best to try to get him in a squad and drive him home, or walk behind him and let him get there without being hit by a car or fall to be injured.

We would get him home (all the while, he swore and threatened us), ring the bell to wake up his older brother, and then make sure he got inside without further incident. This happened nearly every single night.

The pattern was sound. Day shift saw Brian riding his bike around town looking for work and night shift babysat him and made sure he got home alright.

This happened for years. And then one day Brian's brother died.

I was the responding officer who was called to his house at 3 am to see him crying and yelling his brother's name outside on his front lawn.

My partner and I did our best to talk to him in his drunken state, calm him down, and then get him inside where his sick mother had to deal with him. Again…this happened for years until one day, she died.

It was then that the change happened in me.

It was after learning who Brian was and his involvement in the town, that reaffirmed my role as a police officer as one who cares for his community like a shepherd. I had known this concept the entirety of my career. But for the first time, I had seen the role and felt that I had become a true guardian with Brian. Yes, I cared for him and his family deeply.

I felt the change in me come the day that there was no response to my department email that went out to all of the officers, the chief, and the records clerk, asking them for contributions to buy flowers for Brian's mother's funeral. In fact, I felt the change in me start after I heard rumors of some of the officers scoffing at my email while taking their break in the office with the records clerk.

But, I brushed that off.

The change that all of you see now, the "calling out" of bad cops or the demanding the righteous service that we swore an oath to, or all of what you see and feel as criticism coming from me, was that night in September.

I told my trainee, countless times, "We do not arrest Brian."

I told my trainee, "Brian is not to be cited."

I told my trainee, "Make sure you always watch out for Brian, he and his family fall under your protection."

I drilled in his mind over and over Brian's address, his sister's name, his nephew's name and any other information that I thought was crucial to true public service of Brian and his family. And he swore to me that he would respect that.

But I made the change that night when my trainee's partner didn't uphold her oath.

She worked midnights the entire year. She saw Brian day in and day out for nine months. She knew, for the whole nine months that not only was Brian always intoxicated at night, but he never had a headlight on his bicycle. And she had contact with Brian countless times prior to that September night without ever an incident. But it seems that her stats were low that month or she was purposely in need of being malicious. Either way, the vile act of my co-worker and fellow officer, changed the way I viewed the "brotherhood" we all claim we were proud of.

I have no clue why she chose to stop him, but she had every legal right to. I have no idea why she felt the need to place Brian into handcuffs, but she had every legal right to. I later asked my commander how it would have looked on the news if Brian had resisted and the two officers working (neither of whom could fight their way out of a wet paper bag) had to use the Taser on Brian. How would our Chief respond to using a Taser on a subject with mental health concerns? I was told it wasn't my concern.

I also have no idea why this officer decided to write Brian a $25 citation for failure to have a headlight on his bicycle. But she did, and it was legal, regardless of her seeing him for an entire year without one.

And the thing that destroyed my illusion that all cops have compassion was the next morning when Brian's sister called me, told me all of this and then asked me how Brian was supposed to pay for the $250 public intoxication citation the officer had issued him.

I was dumbfounded.

No, politics haven't changed me. What changed me, was when I brought to the attention of my command staff that enforcing public intoxication was not lawful, nor in Brian's case ethical and asked how our department's image as police officers would be seen after this—that completed the transformation inside me.

And instead of discussing the incident or offering Brian's family a solution as community caretakers, I was written up for being insubordinate, for challenging the officer and demanding my commander read the statute that proved we made an illegal arrest.

From that day on, I refused to stand by unethical behavior from police officers. And from that day on, with the feeling that I failed Brian and his family in my heart, I swore that I would never let a cop bully another human being again.

It cost me my job and has made countless other officers question my intent and integrity. But, it also reminds me to hold fast to the oath I swore, to honor all those who came before me and set the example for those to come.

So, for those of you who question my change, debate it, can't understand it or don't agree with it....

All I can say to you is, "Welcome to the change."

The Principles that Changed My Life

1. To prevent crime and disorder, as an alternative to their repression by military force and severity of legal punishment.

2. To recognise always that the power of the police to fulfil their functions and duties is dependent on public approval of their existence, actions and behaviour, and on

their ability to secure and maintain public respect.

3. To recognise always that to secure and maintain the respect and approval of the public means also the securing of the willing co-operation of the public in the task of securing observance of laws.

4. To recognise always that the extent to which the co-operation of the public can be secured diminishes proportionately the necessity of the use of physical force and compulsion for achieving police objectives.

5. To seek and preserve public favour, not by pandering to public opinion, but by constantly demonstrating absolutely impartial service to law, in complete independence of policy, and without regard to the justice or injustice of the substance of individual laws, by ready offering of individual service and friendship to all members of the public without regard to their wealth or social standing, by ready exercise of courtesy and friendly good humour, and by ready offering of individual sacrifice in protecting and preserving life.

6. To use physical force only when the exercise of persuasion, advice and warning is found to be insufficient to obtain public co-operation to an extent necessary to secure observance of law or to restore order, and to use only the minimum degree of physical force which is necessary on any particular occasion for achieving a police objective.

7. To maintain at all times a relationship with the public that gives reality to the historic tradition that the police are the public and that the public are the police, the police being only members of the public who are paid to give full-time attention to duties which are incumbent on every citizen in the interests of community welfare and existence.

8. To recognise always the need for strict adherence to police-executive functions, and to refrain from even seeming to usurp the powers of the judiciary, of avenging individuals or the State, and of authoritatively judging guilt and punishing the guilty.

9. To recognise always that the test of police efficiency is the absence of crime and disorder and not the visible evidence of police action in dealing with them.

Sir Robert Peel wrote these in the 19th century, and they still apply today for modern law enforcement.

For the purpose of my career, my life as a cop and my writings, these have always been known to me as the Nine Principles of Policing by Sir Robert Peel.

Each and every principle can be found in the heart of every story I have written, every call I have relived in the words I have written down, and every moment that comes in my future, regardless of the fact that I am no longer a sworn police officer.

To understand these principles is to face an integrity check every day. Every moment you put on the uniform and every time you mundanely exit your squad to answer a barking dog call, domestic disturbance, subject not breathing or officer down.

Sir Robert Peel and every officer who came before us has paved the way and offered us an opportunity to shine the badge with the courage of the words that formed each guiding principle.

Look, at the end of the day, being a cop is a job. But it is also a part of your name for the rest of your life and those who gave you your name as well as those who will one day have it. It is about adding to your legacy.

Honor your oath, honor the principles and honor those who've done all of that before any of us even took the test to become a cop in the first place.

Chapter Four

WHY DO YOU WANT TO BE A COP?

To date, as hard as I look back on my life and try to pull forth that single moment where I said, "I want to be a cop when I grow up," I can't seem to find any memory of thinking or saying that.

Come to think of it, I don't recall a single moment of decisiveness in my youth where I knew what the hell I wanted to be when I grew up. And although I don't remember ever saying I wanted to be a cop, I can more so support the idea that I probably never did say it.

But, here we are, and as you read this book, I am one. Well, at least at the time of writing this book, I am one. It's December of 2016, and at the very moment I write this sentence, I am on administrative leave…suspension, pending possible termination.

Why? What did I do?

I'll cover the "what" I did later. And hopefully when you read about it, you'll gain a new and deeper appreciation and see some of what police officers go through at the hands of not only the public they interact with but the command staff as well.

Understand something off the bat…this book is 100% PRO POLICE OFFICER, which does include, at times, being anti-command staff. Now, I do not support insubordination, nor any kind of disobedience, however, I do support upholding the oath we all swore and putting the public first. I hope to give you a "behind the 5th wall" look into some of the things that go on within police departments, from my own experience.

I am very much for the concept of "police reform," not that there is a need for one in the way the devil-driven media portrays there to be a need, but more so from the very top down. The fish rots from the head down, and at the very least, I hope this book will open your eyes to not only falling in love again with your police officers but to take a more vested interest in their lives as individuals and as a whole. Bottom line, I want you to get more involved with your local government. I want every town to become a Mayberry.

When it comes to the "why" I was terminated, I am fairly certain it is because of something that I have always been and knew I was long before I became a cop and something that has completely irritated people about me since the beginning of my career…I'm an idealist.

And I recall the very moment that I knew I was one too….

A single police story illustrates and outlines the very core concept of idealism and the frustration that surrounds supporting the very integrity of being an idealist.

It was 2001, my rookie year, and while working the midnight shift, I observed a dark-colored SUV pull out of a bar and travel southbound on one of my town's main roads. The vehicle was traveling south, but it was in the northbound lane doing so.

I followed the vehicle to develop my probable cause. It wasn't that hard to do at all. This vehicle was all over the road, in and out of both lanes. It was either a no-brainer drunk driver or a pretty severe medical condition. I promptly stopped the vehicle, and upon walking up to the driver's side, I knew it wasn't a medical condition. I observed a highly intoxicated male driver pretty much drooped over the wheel of the Jeep.

Within ten seconds of that stop, that driver began to insult me, berate me and talk down to me, you know, the typical anti-cop swearing bullshit from a small man with beer muscles.

At this point in my career, although very early on, it wasn't a new exposure to me. I had arrested drunk drivers before, and some of them were verbally combative. But there was a twist to this one that made the night interesting and my blood boil.

During the traffic stop investigation, I had to call my sergeant over to the stop. It's not that I couldn't handle this myself, rather, the driver presented me with an interesting set of facts that made this stop (at the time) beyond my perceived pay grade. This drunk was a cop. And he was a cop with a gold badge.

The drunk had just left one of the bars in our area after he was celebrating his promotion to sergeant with his co-workers. The irony was disturbing.

The way this police officer spoke to me on the stop was something that I never will forget or forgive. I have seen this cop twice in my career after that moment, and never once has he apologized or said anything about it. But in part, I thank him for helping solidify my views on how we are to act as cops and with one another.

So, after my sergeant arrived on scene I stood by as he "helped" me with the stop (basically taking it over) as he spoke with the driver, used his phone to call someone and then ordered me to drive this drunk male subject to a neighboring town where someone was going to pick him up.

I was ordered to park the drunk's car in the parking lot that was across the street, return to my sergeant with the keys and take the oh-so-pleasant drunk to his destination.

The entire twenty-five-minute drive there I had to listen to this man, this drunk, disrespect me, insult me, call me names and tell me how I didn't know a damn thing about being a cop.

"Fuck you, you rookie. You have no idea what being a real cop is," was one of the insults I remember to this day, and is, in massive part, why I am so critical of my own.

I guess being a "real cop" meant I was supposed to be okay

and agreeable that I was involved with the corruption of the fact that I was transporting this man, this drunk, this brand new sergeant from our county to be picked up by his commanding officer and that no arrest was to be reported and no report was ever to be filed.

Furthermore, I was to be okay with the fact that this drunk was stopped by me after he had left the bar where they were celebrating his promotional party.

To this day, it is one of my biggest regrets for not handcuffing that embarrassment of a man and defying my sergeant and proceeding with the arrest, regardless. And to this day, I have never received an apology from my sergeant, the county or that man himself.

I swore from that moment on that I would stand up and fight every single instance of police corruption that I encountered...and God as my judge, I will. And I am telling you as sure as I write this, it will cost me my job and maybe a hell of a lot more.

As police officers, we are only as honorable as we represent one another in the eyes of those who cast their trusting gaze upon us...you, the public.

I swore to myself that night that I would never again turn the other cheek nor allow others who are around me to when it comes to the concept of tarnishing our badges. I would honor my oath. That oath is everything.

Swearing your name, honor, and integrity, to uphold the Constitution of the United States, the state you are in and thusly vowing to serve, with the highest level of integrity and respect, the very village which adopts you as their own, is the most sincere way of showing love to your fellow man.

Not then nor now have I ever seen that privilege as being otherwise.

Many years after that drunk driving incident, and seemingly all at once, four people I had never met before and one event came into my life and deepened that self-promise I made to hold that standard.

Lieutenant "G.I. Joe" Gliniewicz
Officer Blake Snyder
Melissa Calusinski
And later on, running for Cook County Sheriff and the case of Marni Yang.

Remember those names. Please don't forget them. They changed me, as a cop and as a man, in ways that I did not see coming and it is very important that I get their stories out there. We will be talking about them soon.

For now, my experience on the intolerance of our "brethren" when you run for office like I did, will be saved for another time, as will the case of Marni Yang. I highly suggest you research that case, review the names I speak of in this book and connect the dots for yourself. That's your first detective assignment.

But let's continue with how I got there, first.

WHY DO YOU WANT TO BE A COP?

"Hey! Officer Izzo! I watch your videos and just want to tell you that I want to be a cop, too!"

I get these emails all the time. I love them. It shows such a strong presence of hope and perseverance in a world where men and women still want to become a cop in this day and age, with such media-portrayed hatred against the police. But let me tell you one side of me before we go any further in this book…I am an asshole.

That's right, you read that correctly. Before you write to me, email me, call me, interview me and tell me that you want to be just like me…NO, YOU DON'T.

I have been, several times in my career, someone I regret being. I've been the asshole cop.

I've been the one cop that you see getting in a weaker person's face on a call just because I could.

I've used derogatory slurs, called names, have used my authority to the very edge of its limits just to get what I wanted.

I have never broken a law, but I have been someone that I am embarrassed by.

I've made fun of people, mocked them, belittled them, yelled at them in the lockup to their face and behind their backs. Hell, I've done it in their own homes in front of their families.

I've left those remarks out of my reports (remember that reports are a SUMMATION of the events which happened) and I've downplayed them to command staff. But listen closely…I have NEVER lied.

I've never lied about something I've done when asked directly.

I was, in my youth, the kind of cop that gave us all a bad name. Never doing anything criminal, I've been power-drunk and fueled with an ego that I knew was protected by others and used that protection to push issues as far as I could legally and ethically go. And yes, I am ashamed.

Having and sharing that power is where the mortar is poured that holds the "blue wall of silence" that cops are accused of protecting. The blue wall of silence is a misperceived concept of cops falling under the illusion that the very power they hide behind is the same that will end their careers with certainty.

And for those who say that the blue wall doesn't exist, yes… yes, it does. But it does not exist in the ways that the movies make it out to be. It's much more subtle and common, and it is woven into the false fabric of being a cop.

That blue wall of silence does exist and those who deny it are the ones who count on it being there to hide behind, and it exists every time you give a cop a pass for doing something such as saying the N-word in a joke at a bar.

It exists every time you justify a cop's bad behavior by saying it's because he's not on duty and representing an agency. It exists every time you speed through some other agency's town and flash your badge to get out of that ticket.

Corruption does not end its boundaries where cops plant evidence or lie about facts.

Corruption starts in the smallest cracks in a person's integrity, and there's no getting it back once that dam has been breached.

I have no issue calling out the unethical behavior of other cops. I call my own out constantly and demand that the public and my peers do the very same to me. And it makes me very unpopular with other cops.

The single greatest saying I learned from the academy is, "unaddressed behavior is condoned behavior." And that starts with us.

I call for accountability on the primary level of law enforcement, the patrol officer.

We are NOT mindless drones whose sole dialogue consists of, "just doing my job" in order to bury our conscience and justify immorality, hidden behind an agenda that was written for us and passed along as productive statistics designed to gauge our value as cops, we are POLICE OFFICERS.

And I ask all the time, "Are you a Peace Officer or a Law Enforcer?" Again, I call out the cops.

I cannot call out the urban black youth, whose culture glorifies guns, violence, drugs and killing as the means to propel their status into an almost daily death toll, to stop their behavior, without casting that first light onto my own and call for the same. But that doesn't mean I don't call them out as well. If you listen to my show, you know that it is a nightly occurrence where I openly chastise the black community for their violence.

Draw your sword when the enemy calls for it. But sheath it upon his submission or defeat.

This war between the police and the precious public we serve is winnable and the show of force must come from all sides who are willing to hold the mirror up to their own face and see their reflection as a reminder of what peace looks like. But as police, we have the distinct responsibility of maintaining a first level role to act how the public should. We are the example setters.

I don't remember being trained in the academy on judging others before I measured my own life first.

But I do remember swearing an oath to help those far less fortunate than myself.

Something needs to change in order for the peace we all crave to transpire. And I still believe that we, the police, are the only ones strong enough to take the bold first steps towards setting that example and being that change.

Peace can start with us, but it is fragile and can also end with us so don't let your personal demons put another brick in that wall. We can be the change. So, in knowing that there was that "asshole" part of me, I still always ask one question to any person who tells me they want to be a cop:

"Why?"

I simply ask "why?" and I get the varied array of answers that all sound so textbook and interview-like; all sincere but designed to impress a panel of men and women who sit on a village board and determine if they want to send you to the next step in the hiring process or send you packing.

"I want to serve my community."

"I want to keep the public safe."

"I want to keep bad guys off the streets."

"I want to get more involved in my community and give people the chance I didn't have." And more.

All are great and heartfelt answers, and they truly aren't rehearsed or generic as they really do have a true and profound meaning behind them. After all, you can't reinvent the wheel in a line of questioning and come up with something that the thousands upon thousands before you didn't say first.

But when I ask a person why they want to become a cop, I am looking for a very specific answer that no one has ever given me yet.

I want to hear a fundamental, basic, honest and an almost selfish answer that no one truly thinks about yet it MUST be the basis for why a person wants to become a cop and will be the root of the very type of police officer they become…

The answer I want to hear is simple:

"I want to be a better person."

Your choice in becoming a police officer is the single greatest way, in my opinion, to serve your fellow man, allowing through your service, the chance for YOU to become the best you.

Service to others offers us the greatest opportunity to reach, although never truly possible, our unlimited potential. We must strive for this as men and women, and as police officers, the very nature of this profession offers us the greatest chance to be the best "you."

In my opinion, as a Christian (yes, I am one) that's the whole goal of my time on this earth…to serve Christ by serving others with the gifts He's given me. So, I have been doing my best at it through being a cop. And if He removes me from this profession, I will walk the next path that He sets me on.

It's not without a ton of trial and error, pressure testing, and personal struggle. It's where you feel the pressure testing and problem-solving nature that IS being a cop.

Being a police officer has been one of the most morally challenging roles I have ever played in my life. I have tried to bring my defining characteristics to the title of police officer and not let the title define me, but there have been more than a handful of times when this job has beaten me to my knees and almost to submission…almost.

The academy taught me a lot.

I recall phrases like, "unaddressed behavior is condoned behavior" and "the totality of the circumstances." Both of which I still use as a base of my knowledge to this very day; both having their place and purpose in how every single police interaction is evaluated.

I recall my teachers, my defensive tactics instructors, my lectures on ethics, law, traffic crash reports, etc. All of them.

But you know what I don't recall (I recall they taught us to not use the word "remember")? I don't recall or remember the times we spent in class, talking about when the reality of the role we play kicks in, the real life of it all stacks up like weights on your back and the life of a cop becomes your identity as you lose yourself in the world of your now perceived truth.

My instructors never spoke about the feeling of drowning. They never spoke about the path of the righteous and how ostracizing it is. We were never trained about the subtle betrayals of those who we serve and those we are serving alongside.

There is so much they didn't tell us.... Or maybe they did, and I was just too damn excited to pin that star on my chest and carry that gun around to hear them.

Sixteen years after graduating from the academy (2001 University of Illinois, Police Training Institute Class 1871), my life has been exposed to the most profound growth that a human being could ever ask for. I didn't know that I would become who I am today. Hell, if you told me I would be this man and the way I turned out now, I probably would have had second thoughts and gone back to being a bartender. Nah, I wouldn't have changed anything.

Stories, memories, laughter, pain, pride…I, like everyone who has worn the uniform, have become so much more than who I was when I walked across that stage at graduation from the academy and got my state certificate. I have been molded by the job, shaped by the community and forged by the pressures of what I've seen and done.

But it's not the kind of pressure(s) that you think which I am talking about. It's not the pressure like that of the movies and TV shows, where its high-stress calls, shootings, death, gangs, drugs, car crashes, beaten children and raped women. Sure, it's all of that in some way, but if I told you that those things don't affect us the way you think they should, you wouldn't understand unless you were a cop, nurse, EMS/firefighter, corrections, security or military.

As cops, we are that special kind of breed that can take all of those things and have them processed through our systems as normal or acceptable. Now, I'm not saying that we are inhuman and not affected by the sight of a dead woman who suffocated in a three-gallon pool of her own blood from a ruptured upper GI, but what I am saying is that we process and move on from those things with far greater efficiency than a civilian would. It's just how we are made. God's chosen.

It's the nature of who we are in the moment and how we are able to power forward and serve you.

The pressures of the years that pass are the life-testing pressures that I didn't see coming and what no one told me about.

See, as the years pass, you change, grow, and evolve. It's not a hard concept in any aspect of life to accept. That which does not grow dies.

But I truly feel that so much of me had to die in order to let that growth occur.

You weren't warned in the academy that you would see the absolute worst of mankind in the very people you serve on your tours. You weren't advised that your morality and ethics would be tested and tempted as well as your judgment by those you served with.

No one told me that the very concept of safety and security would be completely removed from those wearing stripes and bars and shiny gold badges, leaving me amongst and sometimes against other police officers on the patrol level and all wondering who we called our guardians.

Understand something…this writing, this work is all meant to do one thing—have you convicted in who you are and why you are a police officer and never have your answer shaken or challenged.

At the very least, I pray to God that you read my words and find some conviction to your own beliefs or verification in your heart of who you are so that you may become MORE of a police officer in order to do more for others.

Make no mistake, I have no answers for you neither in this book or in life. No new insight, methods, law, or tactics. There is nothing that I can improve upon or nothing that will ever be new that someone hasn't already thought of. Someone has already thought of what you just did, done what you forgot to do or come to you for or with an answer on what they or you will do next.

It's the basic concept of life…we live it. But you have the select responsibility of serving those in need and the burden of living a truth in your story that will become the legacy you leave behind.

How you choose to be remembered is entirely up to you. I just selfishly hope that you will somehow make up for my mistakes and failures and that in some way, since we are all part of the brotherhood, my legacy will be righteous and true.
We all need one another. You, them, me…and those we serve. Never forget that.

Chapter Five

FEARLESS AND UNAPOLOGETIC

I wouldn't change a thing for all the gold in the world, but I would have wished that I truly understood what was going to happen to me when I opened my mouth in the first place.

Look, I used to think it was a curse, but now I force myself to see that I was blessed.

I have a mouth on me...always have. And like all Italian mothers say, "He's got a mouth on him, that one." My mother said the same thing about me, growing up.

I am a highly functioning rationally emotionally charged man...and my narrative in life has always been that way. I speak my heart. I am utterly fearless and unapologetic for who I am. One of my favorite sayings is, "when you become fearless, life becomes limitless."

But the balance lies in curbing narcissism and ego with pride in responsibility for serving other men and women without hurting them in the process. Live your truth, but never at the cost of others.

Applying the concept of being "rationally/emotionally vocal" while serving as a cop, has been the most challenging thing I have ever had to evolve with. On the street, my mouth has been my greatest tool getting myself out of many situations that could have required me to use force.

Although I am a powerhouse, trained, skilled and not one to be fucked with, my verbal skills have been far superior to most, and I take great pride in knowing that I can talk anyone into handcuffs without incident. But should a person choose to not fall under my verbal persuasion and want to test my physical ability…well, let's say that I have no issue with that either. After all, the person has their choice.

But it's when the "mouth" meets the "ideals," that is where I have always found the issue. Sometimes (most of the time), it's the command staff that wants that mouth shut. And sometimes (most of the time), it's that I just haven't learned how to do that yet.

'Officer Dominick Izzo' the public figure I was (and in some ways still am) tried to do just that on a daily basis in a different way though. I tried to use my gift and ability to talk to the public in a mass sense thanks to social media, in order to bring us closer together and bridge the gap in our lost community relations. And at the time, I truly felt as if I was doing God's work and spreading respect and love for the community by doing so.

Look, it's no secret that in this time in our history we (the police) are hated. We are no longer in the favor of the general public, bastardized by the urban communities and crucified by the media.

We were scapegoats for the entire Obama presidency and used as beaten advisories for Clinton's 2016 run for office. We took the hate, the blame, the injustice all for one reason…because we are the only ones strong enough to take it. And I say bring on more of it.

So, in 2015, when this all began to surface, I decided to speak out using the platform that is social media.

It was through a massive following of amazing supporters after a simple car-filmed video I did called, "What it truly means when you thank a cop" where I saw the motivation to power forward on a blazing path to aggressively try to be the best version of "me" in order to serve my citizens. A rekindling, if you will, of the cop I wanted to be all while the embers of my law enforcement career started to feel like they were dying out.

Once again, it was by reflecting on the concept that through serving others, I was able to find my path to becoming more. There is beauty in the selfishness of wanting to grow, especially when you find that others benefit from it, too. And I embrace that.

On average, I get anywhere from 100 to 1000 emails each month from the world's most caring, genuine and REAL people, all who tell me that I am what an officer "should be." And I hate that. I am NOT what a cop should be.

My conventional response is that there are so many BETTER cops out there, who far surpass me in ability, knowledge, experience and service, but they are just not as vocal as me.

Please…read this very carefully before you go any further with this book…

I am NOT an inspiration, NOT a model to mold yourself after and NOT someone to admire in this field. I am a very selfish son of a bitch who does not work well with others at times. But that is for a reason.

I value integrity, and at times, I feel the best way to maintain mine is to stay centered and away from the chaos of the daily grind. I am an introvert by nature but appreciate the value of human interaction when it means I get to help others. God forbid I accept help from others, that's a different story in and of itself.

But I am, in fact, no different than you in the fact that I possess no special ability to do what you cannot. I am only a voice who believes with all his heart that there are some unsaid things in this passionate career which must be said before my time is over. And in doing so, it has already cost me my job twice and the third time is looming around the corner.

My thoughts are always this as a reply: find your way to be unique and irreplaceable, but able to continue to serve in ways that challenge and improve you.

Do not fall on the sword as I have. The people will not benefit from their loss of you, and you will find yourself on the same island of isolation that I have come to know too well.

I learned, too late and perhaps still haven't learned, that my ego is far more destructive than any tool or weapon on my duty belt or in my armory. But I have justified my actions as an explosion, clearing the path for the righteous ones, such as you, to march ahead and go where I cannot.

So, let me repeat that…I am NOT the model of a cop, nor was I ever, nor will I ever be…. Who I am is a blazing light that shines for you to see all of who you are without the shadows.

I want you to see the utter best of you, the epitome of your potential and I want you to surpass me as a human in every way possible. That is my calling, to make you better, even if I have to drag you kicking and screaming to see your ability.

You are the one who decided to become a cop. And you now have to understand that you must bring your absolute best to the table every single day, or you are utterly worthless. Have this mindset, embrace the pressure and standards, and force yourself to attain this daily goal. It will be and is worth it.

There are INFINITE numbers of other officers out there who far surpass my status of what the model/mold of a police officer should be like. And they are the ones who, like I said, I model myself after. These cops, the ones that I have known, served alongside with and modeled myself after, are the reason I am so vocal about law enforcement. I want to do them proud in the only way I truly feel I know how.

And that said, "Officer Dominick Izzo" is all that he is because of them, my family and God. And the man I am now and strive to be as I fight forward will be in direct reflection of honoring them as well as God for giving me the privilege to do so.

THE SOCIAL MEDIA MACHINE

Officer Dominick Izzo (the social media persona) came about after the death of Lt. Charles "G.I. Joe" Gliniewicz.

Gliniewicz was a police officer lieutenant for the village of Fox Lake, Illinois, who committed suicide on September 1st, 2015. I will talk about this case later and the issues and impact it had on me.

In October of that same year, I was walking out of one of the gas stations in our town, on duty, and someone extended their hand to shake mine. They simply said, "I want to thank you for your service." That was the third person that day.

Prior to our knowledge of Gliniewicz committing suicide, it was thought that he was murdered by three suspects, who were still at large. The surrounding communities had grown to such a level of tightness and a sense of neighboring that I had never seen before and people were suddenly interacting with us police more than ever.

So, I wanted to talk about the impact that a simple "thank you" had on me, coming from the perspective of the cop who received it.

I did the very first video on my Facebook page on what it truly means when you thank a police officer, it was massively viewed and shared, and the rest was history.

The video was shared on several police forums, police websites, and countless personal pages.

I started gaining international attention for my direct, outspoken, passionate, and very controversial views over the reality of law enforcement and the interaction with the public that we serve. Bottom line, I was one of the first active-duty cops who told the truth about how I felt, and people loved it.

Risk and reward has yet to be determined, but I am one of the only police officers in the country who is not only willing to say but IS saying what others want to…and I have no idea why this is. THAT infuriates me.

More cops need to open their mouths, period.

The result of this risk I've taken while voicing my views in my own law enforcement community is that I am respected in private by my peers but hated in public by them. Remember what

I said about that island of ostracism? Cops do have a gang mentality at times and do gang up on their own.

Many cops do privately email me or call me, talking about the stress of the injustices they see but that they won't speak out against what is happening due to fear for losing their jobs and their pensions. I can only say that I understand the leverage that is held over them but do not respect the fact that they will not speak up. In some way, this is violating the oath and dishonoring the badge.

They also cite their inability to articulate their expressions the way I do, their being reserved or their lack of caring or even jealousy but for me (let's face it, they just aren't abrasive assholes like I am).

It's very frustrating and sad to me that police officers will not stand up for themselves in this trying time of publicly-misguided scrutiny, fueled by media lies, politics and even more so that they won't stand up and support me.

But this issue of scrutiny has now been created out of being silent and unwilling to defend ourselves and is what is going to destroy us in the end. One of my favorite sayings that I learned in the academy was, "unaddressed behavior is condoned behavior." Well, warriors, when police don't address the lies that are being ruthlessly spread about them, they are allowing it. NOT the street cop as much as the command staff.

But going back to other cops not being so willing to speak out, I understand and respect the apprehension, as this, of course, has been due to the past and current practice of department discipline, media demonizing, threats from the public and much more. It's a load of bullshit that keeps the good cops silent and gives that illusion of having a blue wall to protect others.

As far as myself and why I risk speaking up? You have to keep in mind that I am not married, have no children, and am not afraid to put myself out there for public display and attack. I may seem "career foolish," but it is necessary to have this mindset when taking on the fight that I willingly choose.

But more than that I truly believe that if we are given the gift of life, we must live it to our greatest potential. If I have passion for police officers, integrity, honor, pride, and truly serving my community, what is that saying about me if I do not speak out? I can't and won't live like that.

It has cost me dearly in my personal life, just for maintaining who I am. I have lost friends and truly loving relationships at the inability for some to not support or understand why I just can't go with the flow.

So, in the end, if I take the hits for my brothers and sisters in blue and get the ax again, so be it…. I will gladly go down, swinging for all of us.

My only hope is that someday, some of those who were quick to open their mouths in judgment against me will take a look at what I really was trying to do for them this whole time.

FREEDOM OF SPEECH

Here is something that needs to be understood and accepted right now:

The police DO NOT have the right—the same freedom of speech as you as citizens do under the First Amendment no matter what the courts say. I will argue tooth and nail with you if you think we do and prove to you the court of public opinion says otherwise.

We aren't even allowed to say words that are now part of the American culture (and if you don't know what I am referring to, then just listen to any rap song) without being heavily disciplined or even terminated.

But human expression is key to our individual, dynamic, and necessary identities, regardless that we wear the same uniform and are all called "police officer." And that same expression is necessary for the betterment and healing of the relationship between the police and the public.

If only one side of this relationship between the public and the police is allowed to fully express themselves, then there will be a continuance to this great divide with severe consequences in the future. And it's happening as we speak, just log online or watch the news…apathy from the police. But the perpetuate conundrum is that the police will never stop caring about the community, no matter how hard they are beaten.

The primary self-expression and "dialogue" of the police has been through arrest, citation, summons, detainment, jailing and seizures; although NECESSARY as a means to the ends, this method has proven to be the catalyst of a public disdain for police due to the fact that the very nature of this dialogue has always been at the guise of "just doing my job." More so, the only kind of conversations being reported by the media, which the public digests, is that cops arrest people, period.

The primary dialogue between them SHOULD be back to the roots where service, conversation, connection, and community are the paramount focus, and that should be reported by the media.

The older I grow, the more I see through the eyes of those I have served.

Be it through a righteous arrest or an act of officer discretion, I foolishly believed that the public was already aware of why the police do what we do. Oh, how I was mistaken. All it takes is a thread of comments on some social media police video post, and the distorted truths come out.

Again, thanks to the false narrative of the media and the indoctrination of those who are too blind to do their own thinking, we, the police have been serving under a set of rules and law that is just not explained to the people we are governing. Basically, we take away people's freedom at times without educating them why.

Look, if you speed down my town's road at 45 mph and the speed limit is only 25 mph, you can't claim "I didn't know" as a viable defense to get out of a citation.

But if you resist a police officer and display a knife and that officer shoots you, and you argue, "Why did the cop use a gun?!

That man only had a knife!" Then this is where education needs to be done to teach people the WHY behind police tactics and training.

In part (and I fully hold command staff accountable) we are to blame for the public not understanding why we use force, arrest, etc. Why have we not educated them?

My fear, my greatest fear is that which happens when one side of a pair in a relationship stops caring in that relationship.... When one side says they are tired of how we do not hear their needs and then the relationship abruptly dissolves. When that happens, the relationship ends, and life goes on. But with the relationship between the public and the police, if that relationship ends, chaos follows.

As police, we cannot afford to let this happen, and again, WE are the ones strong enough to prevent this from happening. But I fear that one day, the price for all the media lies and the lack of education on the public will lead to the loss of caring by the police.

When you are emotionally/physically abused, taken for granted, left to do all the work, not appreciated, constantly disrespected in your relationship, when this happens, and we've had enough, we all walk away.

Or in the case of communities such as the black, urban, uneducated, fatherless, male youth, they resort to the only known expression that makes them feel heard and powerful...violence. Non-racially motivated for this point, yet relatable for another topic at another time, the language of violence is powerful.

I am, however, singling out the black urban youth at this time for the simple fact that no group has more erroneously and incorrectly challenged the integrity of the very men and women who serve them, the police.

They have done so out of ignorance, lack of education, and the failure of the Democratic Party which keeps them held at a victim's stance with only one option to escape their reality... blame someone. Blame the police.

This narrative and dialogue can be discussed at length, but for the sake of a simple and powerful concept, for years the black urban youth have felt neglected and abused and without the necessary relating that needed to be done or educating that needed to be done to see the truth. They are now left with a radical and almost religious fanatical like belief that all cops are against them. It borders the concept of religious extremity.

The truth can be no further to see than in the actions that are right in front of them and in how we truly serve them, and so many of them in their own community know this. It is not a racial plight, but rather, a fatherless, youth, and MALE-based issue.

That is not what I am focusing on in this book. But it is a parallel to how we, as police, have been left to carry this relationship burden on our own while serving both sides of the government and the people. We are the ultimate tightrope walkers with a stack of dishes in each hand that is constantly adding up on each varying side…one small shift and we fall, taking them all with us. And we won't let that happen. All the while, the media keeps shaking the cable we are walking on.

And in the end, all relationships are not 50/50…they are 100/100. And in my strong, personal opinion, the public has not been showing us how much they care; nor will they. Millennial upbringing has shown that they just don't feel they need to. Hell, that's the key issue right there. Millennials are taught to FEEL and not THINK.

But that is ok…like any strong person in a relationship, we the police will continue to set the example of how to lead. And we will educate the public through example and action.

Use your speech with passion, truth and righteousness, and you will be heard.

Chapter Six

DON'T BECOME A COP—JUST DON'T...UNLESS

This is, by far, the absolute worst time in the history of policing to be a police officer.

If you are considering this path as a career choice, reconsider it immediately. I mean it. Do not fill out that application, don't pay the $30 fee, don't show up to the physical test, the written test...just don't do it.

Don't practice a speech in the mirror for what you think they'll want to hear in the interviews. As a matter of fact, just forget about it.

Forget about the interview(s), the polygraph, the psyche test, etc...this job is so not worth it. You'll hate it.

You will be called a racist, a robot, a non-compassionate revenue generator, road pirate, and more for the state. You'll be called a corrupt alcoholic, a womanizer or bull-dike if you are female, power hungry, and an insecure person who couldn't get a real job and so much more.

You'll be labeled a wife-beater (and I am not married) an alcoholic like I said (I RARELY drink) and a criminal. Don't ask me why, either. I have no idea where all of this comes from other than I have heard that some people think that cops beat their wives and get away with it as well as drink and drive and never get arrested. But, there is some truth to the power of the badge and its delusional blue wall of silence which I will get into later.

As a cop, you will be hated in Vermont for something that another cop did in Wyoming, even though you have never heard of him or met him. And that cop who did that thing in 1993, well, you'll pay for it in 2017 just because someone read about it online. We are all the same in the public's eye, no matter how different you try to be.

Doesn't matter if you are like me, a male who's 5'7", 200 lbs. with grey hair, blue eyes and is white, but that female officer who's 5'3" and 110 lbs., brown hair, brown eyes and is black, will have done something to someone and that person will have told another and that little game of "telephone" will make all cops out to be the bad guys in the end. What one cop does all are accountable for.

You will be faced with commanders who seem to have it out for you because of some personality conflict you've no doubt created, citizens who absolutely have it out for you because they hate what you represent and family and friends who never can relate or understand what "having it out" for you means to you and will just say, "Well, you chose that job."

And the stress…dear God, the stress. I could write a whole book about the stress that stems from the job, but I need to stay on track. All I will say is that there is the concept of throwing a pebble in the water and it starting a tidal wave. Well, as far as law enforcement goes, it will not be a pebble in the water, but rather a chunk of Mt. Everest that was thrown into the sea by Thor and the tidal wave that will affect your life as a whole, will be the most destructive tsunami you've ever experienced.

But again, we are the ones who remain after the waters recede.

As it was told to me once before when I was new at this job, "Buckle the f' up."

To recap, if you haven't figured it out by now, being a police

Don't Become A Cop—just Don't...unless

officer is, by far, the worst job on the planet...DON'T DO IT.

Now...

If you still, regardless of what I've said, feel in your heart of hearts that you are called to be a police officer for the reason of making a difference in our world, then, proceed.

If you are the type of man or woman that never backs down from a challenge, loves to show the world the best of your integrity and character, especially when it's being challenged under fire and service to others and it is your passion...then being a police officer is not a job for you, it's who you were meant to be.

If you are an idealist, passionate, live by truth and righteousness in that you are the very backbone in which your community will test their strength, then you are the cop we want, and you will find yourself in the most honorable of services.

But hear me clearly...this job, this path, this passion is about SERVICE.

It is about making the difference your heart is telling you that you MUST make with every beat of it. Don't seek to wear the uniform and be authoritarian. Don't seek to do the blood spatter testing after watching some television show because you now want to be in forensics. Don't think or do this job for stolen auto pursuits, shoot outs, bar fights or stumbling on hidden kilos of cocaine in car door jams....

Don't do this job for any reason other than your soul was created to help people...PERIOD.

Being a cop is not a job, it's the most honored position in life where you get to be the best human being in the world, despite all kinds of horrible challenges from both your community as well as your command staff, in order to help those who need your help. Understand this now, you will be pressure tested. But that's exactly what law enforcement is—Pressure Testing and Problem Solving.

But, pressure is what makes diamonds, and the strongest steel is forged in the hottest flames. Being a police officer is extreme pressure and will offer you an opportunity to bring out the best in who you are for both the community and YOU.

That is also what law enforcement is, an opportunity for greatness from within. And greatness starts with love. You MUST love the people you serve. Wicked or righteous, criminal or victim, you must love your neighbor as yourself and be the peace in force that God called you to be through your state-granted authority.

You can't give what you don't have. This job is about love, believe it or not. We have to have love, even for the darkest of evils that we will come across. For evil can only be defeated with love. And in order to defeat the evil and protect yourself, you will have to love who you are as a man/woman and the officer you swear you will be.

You must bring that love to your tour every day. We need police officers, men and women who love our nation and the towns we serve. We need them to love our citizens…ALL OF THEM, no matter how they act or behave. You are the one they will need, encounter, call upon, count on, hate, lie to, trust…you will have a relationship with all of them, and relationships are based out of love. You must be the one to love, regardless of being loved.

And here's the deal, you will be the one who needs the relationship more than the citizens will. You will need them to love as a means to define yourself. They will be the canvas in which you paint your art on, and the world will recognize your style through them. Their love, regardless of how conditional, fleeting, or obtuse, will be your reward and your means to constantly redefine yourself.

So, never say or think for one second that you don't need those people…you do. You are nothing without the people you serve and the reflection in their eyes—how they see you—is everything.

Also, understand this now and live its truth…there is a massive difference between being a Cop and a professional Police Officer.

Yes, I identify myself as a cop here and there, but my title, role, passion and integrity is in being a Police Officer and representing my town, people, and self as such. You need to think of yourself as a professional police officer, a man/woman who exudes integrity and character and earns the title that so many of us have identified with and worked hard to keep held in the highest regard before you came along.

A cop does the job, but a Police Officer IS the job. And when you discover the meaning in that, you will have learned that this is just the opposite of what I dissuaded you from and this is truly, the greatest time in history to become a police officer with every moment being yours to prove that so.

THE ENVELOPE

When I saw that the return address marking on the envelope was from the police department I had just tested for, I immediately felt my stomach drop.

Envelope in hand, I literally stood there at the mailbox in my condo complex and didn't move. I just looked at the upper left-hand corner where "Round Lake Beach Police Department" was typed and felt my heart pounding in my chest. The stress that I was holding in my hand was immeasurable.

What you have to understand when I say "the stress" is that the stress up to this point (as far as interviewing and testing went) was beyond overwhelming, and I had no clue that just holding a letter from the police department would ever feel so heavy in my hands. The envelope represented a four-week process of pressure, dropping my work schedule to adhere to testing and interviews, polygraph testing, office lobby waiting times, handshaking total strangers over and over, looking and acting my best and much more.

Rejection…I assumed nothing but rejection was in that envelope.

After all, all I heard from all of the cops I had known was how they tested three, five, nine times before they got hired. So,

I expected nothing less than that when I opened the letter from my first testing attempt.

    I opened it without hesitation, and at the moment I read the opening sentence, "Dear Mr. Izzo, we are proud to offer you the position of police officer to the…" I fell back onto the couch, dropped the letter, and openly wept…HARD. I was relieved.

    Understand something… those weren't tears of joy or happiness. They were tears of purged frustration over waiting on this letter, the stress of interviews and testing, worrying about changing/not changing career paths, etc. It was incredibly overwhelming.

    I had been going through the process of getting hired as a police officer for several weeks, and within those weeks, I put a lot of stress and expectations on myself. I demanded of myself that I show that I was qualified to be a police officer, and I was not accepting anything less than being hired. I visualized and wanted to manifest it.

    Now, I know what some of you are thinking, "weeks!? I spent YEARS testing."

    If you are someone who has never tested for a police department before or are thinking about it, please just let me say that the process is painstaking, stressful and at times accompanied by a sense of hopelessness. After all, your fate rests in the hands of people who judge you mostly on the vibe they get from you and the basis of your past.

    For those who have tested, I don't mean to or want to "brag" about this, but from the first day I dropped off my application until the day I was accepted was four weeks…and on my very first test. I took one other test during that time and was also offered a job, but took my first department's offer.

    I was an anomaly. From the time I dropped off my very first application to the moment I got my letter offering me a police officer position, was again, four weeks… Yes, FOUR weeks on my first submission. But I appreciated and valued the process as it was an eye-opener to see what other men and women had repeatedly gone through.

That stated up front, never once, in all my years of being a cop, have I ever taken that for granted and I think about it all the time. I always recognize that although the spot was mine through visualization, manifestation and God-predetermined, there could have been others out there who were incredible and who could have done the job as well, if not better than me. For this, any one of you who I may have gotten the spot over, I am forever appreciative and will never let you down.

I talk about this because I know the stress that so many others have gone through, for countless years as they tested and got rejected from the job they were so passionately hoping to get. I have heard the stories and seen the looks on their faces after those rejection letters were opened. I just need you to know that I value you as well.

I know the tears of frustration and the constant questioning of, "why" that a person who's testing will ask themselves when that letter of rejection comes in the mail.

"Why" not them? Truth is, you won't know. Something, somewhere along the lines during the testing process, you just weren't seen as a good fit for the department you tested for and their needs. Don't take it personally, regardless of it being extremely personal, but this means that there is a different path you must take and power forward. It's a relationship, and like all relationships at one point, we don't fit in.

That said up front, please know, if you are in the process of testing to be a police officer and do not get accepted, understand that this may not be the answer you want, but it is an opportunity and a path that you must look at as yours to make a difference elsewhere. This job is not for everyone, and this life could just be something that does more harm to you than good.

It's in the pages of this book that I want to give MY experience in being a police officer so that you may have a slight view into the world that we live in. Again, this is my view, my experiences, and will never be yours. But we can all relate on some level and it is my hopes that you will at least read my passion for the path I have chosen, my loyalty to the profession I am in and my dreams for a better future based on the actions I take, each and every day I hold the honor of my title…Police Officer.

WHAT'S THE POINT OF EVERYTHING SO FAR?

I didn't want to be a cop, or at least back then, I don't recall having that typical inner draw to the appeal of the badge, uniform and gun, like most youth seemed to. Unlike others I knew, mine was never the "I wanna be a cop!" attitude or mentality, however, I craved for a greater sense of purpose that what I had been doing up until that point. I just didn't know what it was.

I was a bartender.

I was extremely happy as a career bartender. Well, not extremely happy, but I was really damn good at it, made great money and literally was paid to play for a living.

But I think, even though I didn't admit it to myself back then, that there was this missing piece of me that needed to contribute to the world, more than just getting people drunk and showing them a good time.

For as far back as I can recall, I always felt incomplete, and my job(s) defined most of who I was. But being a bartender, although honorable, just was not fulfilling to my soul. I felt I needed to become more of myself. So, I will say, that is when I started to feel "the calling."

I used to have fits of little identity crisis. "Who am I?" "Is this your best?" "Is the world a better place because of you?" I would feel the pull of truly *knowing* in my whole body, that there was so much more of me, and I was not living to my potential. But the question that I just couldn't answer was "how?"

But those same voices would fuel my inner conflict and reply, "Yeah, but look at all this money you have…and all those women…" and of course the little boy in me would be pacified for a while with all those worldly goods as the man inside of me was pounding at the front door of integrity, ordering me to let him in...and in the end, the man kicked the door down and took over.

But again, I didn't want to be a cop for all of those common reasons you hear so many others talk about. I didn't want to be some crime scene investigator. I didn't want to be a detective or an FBI special agent. I didn't want to be any singled-out part of law enforcement, I just knew that I wanted to help the world in some way.

Things started very rapidly, and the comments came on how "you'd make a great cop." One night a bar patron told me, as I passed him a beer, "you look like you should be a cop." And for weeks, one after another, the remarks would come on how I looked like a cop, spoke like a cop, had the presence of a cop and so on.

There was an older man, who was one of my favorite afternoon patrons, who heard a lot of this in passing and just said to me one day, "I told you pally, just go take the test."

And the final straw was my friend Wendy. She had been a cop for a year and one night just kind of pushed me over the edge and told me that I was wasting my talent as a bartender, that I would make a great cop and that I would regret it if I let the chance pass.

To this day, I still thank her for pushing me towards my career path. And if you are reading this, sister, I am glad I listened to you and proud to have served the same county and state with you, but even prouder to call you family all these years.

So, in February of 2001, I took my first test.

I thought that by becoming a police officer, I would meet my inner need's idealistic nature of trying to better the world in a way that suited me. Had I known that in becoming a cop, I would have been helped more than I seemed to have helped, I would have done so much sooner.

Sixteen years later and I think I have just started to crack through the first layer of the foundation of what being a police officer truly means and I am not sure if I will ever know it all.

It is my deepest hope to know that by trying to discover the true nature of being a cop, that someone's life was impacted in a positive way from the work done. But if not, I will just keep on trying. One thing is for certain, in those sixteen years, my life was profoundly impacted, and I will never be the same.

Chapter Seven

THE ACADEMY

Alright, let's get this out of the way right now; I cried my first night at the academy. You bet your ass I did. I was straight out stressed and fucked up in the head out of my comfort zone.

I will be as open, blunt, direct, and honest as possible in this book. If you haven't already seen my truth come through in my videos and other writings, or are introduced to me for the first time, I am all about integrity, truth and having my actions match my words. And I am going to let you have it all.

Having never been away from home or even gone to college, my first night in that academy dorm room was spent crying and second-guessing my decision.

I started wondering if I could call my now former boss and get my job back? Would my girlfriend still wait for me three months from now until I got back in town? (Just wait until we get to the part in my story how being a cop destroyed my relationship.)

What about my pets, would they even survive without me for that long? (Yes, someone was caring for them, but I was having a massive pity party for myself.) What about my friends? My life in general, would it even be the same anymore?

I literally had my 2001 Motorola Startac flip phone, open and ready to hit the send button to call my now former boss and ask for my job back…. I was not afraid, I was terrified of the choice I had made and how the unknown was right in front of my eyes.

I sat on this incredibly hard and small dorm room mattress, looked out the window into the dark night sky, and felt the anxiety build in my chest. My whole world was changing, and I was beyond outside of my comfort zone. That bar, those people, those "friends" were my daily routine and my safe place. I felt that I could not get through this, and I have never wanted to run back to safety so fast in my whole life.

I tried to justify every single angle and excuse on that first night as to why I needed to leave and go home. All the testing, interviewing, new suit purchases, polygraphs, psych testing, and weeks of stress meant nothing at that moment.

I was so far out of my comfort zone and so deep into fear that I just wanted to pack up and leave. But, as you already know by now, I didn't. I powered through.

I put the phone down, turned out the light, set the alarm for 0430 hrs., and forced myself to go to bed. And I cried my eyes out. I wasn't sad…I was terrified of change.

That night I learned a very personal life lesson. To this day, when I go through something very personal in the realm of change when I struggle and have an inner war, I think of that night, and how I pushed, pulled and powered through, and the end results have been amazing. I loathe change to the point I crave it. Someday that will make sense to you. But to me, it is a welcome fight, even when I know I am going to get hit hard.

ACADEMY LIFE

Monday through Friday… Up at 0430 hrs. for 0500 PT, breakfast by 0700 hrs. and class at 0800 hrs. until 1700 hrs. And damn that fifty-something-year-old cop, who was our PT instructor and his "bicycles" abs exercise. That guy was in amazing shape and put us all to shame, but he loved to torture us, daily! I respect the hell out of him.

The Academy

The academy was very structured with education and practical knowledge of the job, but what it was, more so, was responsibility and the representation of who doesn't have the fortitude to be a police officer. And that came through in the daily pressure testing of just going to class.

I was shocked at how many classmates I had that just didn't understand who we were.... We were there training to be THE police yet so many just did not act like it.

For example, we had these daily class evaluations that needed to be filled out after every class. Didn't matter if we had the same instructor, back to back, but we had to fill out evaluations each and every single hour.

It was shocking how many people would bitch and complain, "Ugh, why do we have to fill this out every single time!?" yet it didn't dawn on them that this was conditioning us for the very nature of what we'd be doing over the next twenty years... PAPERWORK.

Or curfew. We had a 2000 hrs. (8pm) curfew every night. Apparently, the graduating class before ours abused the hell out of the college campus nightlife, and a curfew was instituted for our class and the future recruits.

It took about five weeks before it was abused and someone paid the price. Prior to this week five, though, I was completely and utterly shocked at how many of my classmates would stay out past curfew and then brag about it IN CLASS the next day. I never said anything, but looking back, I am irritated at myself for not calling them out. We should be counted on, from the very beginning, to hold each other to the highest standards, which are expected from us. This is a part of why I say the hiring process needs to be thoroughly looked into.

But back to week five and the curfew.

All I remember was it was 2200 hrs., and one of my roommates was not back yet.

Apparently, a whole group of recruits decided to give the instructor staff a big old middle finger and stay out late drinking at one of the local bars.

The story goes that they were all walking back to the dorms and being a bit louder than they should have, getting the attention of other campus college students who were trying to sleep/study, thusly resulting in someone calling the police.

So, the police come and approach the intoxicated group of my fellow recruits and make contact, starting their investigation. It was during this moment of pure, poorly-judged phrasing that one of the recruits cuts the officer off by holding his hand out as he approached and said, "Hey, man…I'm a cop."

The next day in class was pretty cut and dry for those of us who saw what was coming. Honestly, I really don't have to go into too much detail. I was embarrassed for what this "fellow" new officer did, and I am glad he paid the price.

The Monday after we got back from the weekend, having Thursday being the night this happened, is when an outcome was determined by the teaching staff of the academy. We were allowed to go home each Friday night, and unbeknownst to us, an investigation was conducted, departments were called, and a verdict was reached.

I remember the one guy, who was the center of the incident, walking in from the head instructor's office back into our classroom to get his books off his desk. He stood there for a moment, finally serious after all his time in class joking around and told the class, "Don't screw around. They mean business here." And with that, he walked out.

And we never saw him again.

And from that little life lesson of accountability, I wish it would be noted by everyone reading who's entering the academy, that you are not the police yet, nor are you not NOT the police either. You are stuck right in the middle of looking like the police by uniform, but not able to do jack shit yet. You are ambassadors who are fortunate enough to be trained and trusted to be the police. So, start acting like it from day one.

LEARNING

Learning was a dynamic process in the academy. The classroom was balanced by lots and lots of practical-application training. And to this day I remember my training as it was burned in like classical conditioning.

Day one for tactics training was a real eye-opener for me, and I suppose it was designed that way by the instructors to be so. Regardless of their intent, it worked, and I am very respectful of my training.

We were all in this warehouse, which was retrofitted for a classroom's needs. We had the range there, scenario training rooms, role-play rooms, etc. All of our hands-on and tactics training was done at this ranch.

The very first day, we were given paintball helmets and paintball guns. We were only wearing out academy clothes too. I was in slacks, academy polo and an academy sweatshirt.

The instructor grabbed us by two's and each pair took a turn on one of three set up scenarios. We were given the orders not to discuss what had happened when we returned, allowing each new pair to experience the scenarios without readied awareness.

Pair by pair, they returned after only a few minutes, with stains of water on their clothes, welts on their skin and looks of complete and utter defeat on their faces. The orders were again to remain silent until all pairs were finished going through the training.

After several minutes, it was my turn.

A female recruit and I were led outside and into the parking lot. There were cars all over and a large building with numerous unmarked doors. This was all part of the warehouse building on the ranch, but again, this was scenario training, and I had no clue what to expect.

The instructor, a very large man who was a retired cop, simply said, "Through those doors, there is an armed robbery in progress. Take all the time you need and deal with it." Then he walked away. No further instruction and no questions were allowed to be asked.

Before you read further, just stop for ninety seconds and ask yourself what you would do or how you would process all of this, because that's less than the time we took to process and plan and I can still feel how confused I was back then to this day.

So, confused, unsure, but willing to become confident, we walked towards the door. I was expecting role players to walk out and engage us at any moment. I had my "pistol" aimed at the door, and we approached slowly.... I was shaking.

Once we got to the door, the plan was simple. The door opened outwards, with the knob on the right. I told my partner to open the door and get to the left of it, and I would enter. She nodded in agreement, took her position, turned the knob, cracked the door open and...

"Fuck!"

I felt the entire portion of my right arm completely throbbing and burning as if someone had just taken a sword out of a blacksmith's fire and slid it over the back of my arm.

"Hold! Scenario over!" is what we heard the instructor yell next.

I turned, looked over my right, and saw another instructor/role player, sitting in one of the cars in the lot. He had a pistol pointed at me, and he was the "getaway driver" that we hadn't bothered to even check for on our approach. And to make matters worse, they didn't use paintballs. They used these hard, plastic, water-filled projectiles that completely reinforced classical conditioning in us. I walked right past my own death.

We returned to the classroom, de-briefed, and began our 12 weeks of tactical training.

To this day, I never approach a scene without looking into all the cars.

CLASSROOM STUDY

It is in the academy classroom, and at the ranch, you learn the fundamentals of being a cop. You learn the law, the formula for law such as custody plus questioning equals Miranda.

You learn 4th Amendment laws, search and seizure, state laws, how to write traffic crash reports, domestic violence and the evolution of how the laws have increased to protect victims.

You learn basic level defensive tactics, or as I referred to it, bullshit. (Keep in mind that a very large portion of my life has been spent in physical skills development and I am very biased when it comes to training.)

You will learn how to position your squad car on a traffic stop and the emergency red and blue light usage during both the day and night shifts.

You'll learn about mentally ill subjects, paperwork, juvenile laws, flashlight usage, concealment versus cover, domestic role play, public complaint role play, theft role play, role play on top of role play and lots and lots of firearms training.

The academy had us thinking we were ready and built our confidence very high. And I am glad it did.

It was 12 weeks of fitness, education, firearms and so many other aspects of the job that we were conditioned to think very black and white about the job, in general, in that everyone wanted to kill us and nothing was ever routine.

I remember thinking that on every call, everything had to be done very structured-like and that also like I said, everyone was intending to kill me. That's how much they pounded officer safety in our heads.

What I ultimately learned from the academy was not to take the job lightly, and it wasn't black and white, it was completely grey.

I learned to always respect the fact that I went through twelve weeks of an education that so many others wanted, and I was fortunate enough to get. I saw the world through a different lens of responsibility, yet I still didn't see myself as a "cop" due to the fact that I had not yet earned that place in the world.

After twelve weeks, a walk across a stage and a handshake from my new chief, I was ready to take on the world as a new member of my department...but I still didn't consider myself a police officer yet only because I had not felt, inside of me, that I had the honor that so many others earned. I had a very long way to go.

INSIGHT

When I left the academy, I knew full well that the job wouldn't be what we were training for. I knew that we were getting the shock and awe within twelve weeks that would prepare us for the dynamics of the job in general, but not the raw emotional backing of, "Hey...I'm a police officer now."

I won't lie, it took a long time for it to register in my head that I was, in fact, a police officer.

It took Greg, my FTO, to tell me, "Sign your name with your title on your reports" because I was signing my name "Dominick Izzo" and not "Ofc. Izzo." It just took a long time for me to comprehend that I had the right to associate myself with so many other men and women who truly earned this right that I was working myself into.

Chapter Eight

MY FIRST NIGHT ON PATROL

What you have to understand is that the academy conditioned us (well me at least) that everyone, on every call, that you will ever interact with was going to shoot and kill me and I will say this over and over again.

Some may chalk this up to conditioned paranoia, I chalk it up to excellent conditioning education by the instructors for "officer awareness" through excellent training. But it wasn't so much "awareness" as it was paranoia on day one for me.

And what a day that was.

I was sent to Midnight shift (mids) my first month of field training, or FTO as it's called. Traditionally, it seems, most new officers get sent to the later shifts as the older officers with seniority always want day shifts, making things easier for life I assume. (But later in your career you actually bid for midnights to be as far away from the command staff as possible.)

Being in the FTO program, I was exposed to all three shifts in my department, but 2300 hrs. to 0700 hrs. was my first starting point.

It was summer, end of June, hot and it was my very first time wearing all of the equipment that a cop has to wear for an extended period of time.

Duty belt with all the tools, bulletproof vest, heavy boots, thick polyester blend clothing that just sealed in all the heat and sweat. It was an additional 40 lbs., of weight in equipment.

All of this made for a new experience for me with all of the little things secured on my person all at the same time, and for so long. This was much different than the academy, especially since I had a fully loaded firearm on my hip at all times now.

Walking, bending over to pick up a dropped pen, sitting in a car comfortably, eating, etc., all these daily life tasks were all very challenging now. When you first wear the uniform, it's a pride thing. But after you try to function in it, you quickly start asking yourself the necessary questions like, "Crap…can I run in this if I do have to chase someone?" or "How the hell do guys jump over fences in the movies in this stuff?" or even, "How the hell do I reach for my water bottle that just fell on the other seat?!"

So, keeping all of that in mind I am not going to place blame on what happened on the 40 plus pounds of additional gear, but I won't deny its contributing factors to my night, either. For that, I will only blame me.

*****

Look, I said it was hot out, remember? I mean, HOT. Yes, I know the sun wasn't out; it was after 1 am. I will make all kinds of excuses for what happened to me, but it's northwest suburban Chicago, and we all know that summer here gets humid and lousy. Some Chicago summer nights are just muggy and crappy. This was absolutely one of them.

The call came out after 1 am. I had been riding around with my FTO Greg since a little after 11 pm. We did the "first-day" things that a new FTO and his trainee do, prior to getting in the squad and going out on the road.

We drove around the town, talked about expectations and the field training program itself, etc. Greg gave me his history with the department, his expectations, and his offering of mentorship in that he wanted me to succeed. Greg was one of the best training officers I have ever known.

We backed a few officers up on traffic stops, toured the problem areas, and I got an initially geographical acclimation of the town. I reviewed my FTO manual and a few department policies while Greg got coffee or used the bathroom. Overall, it was a slow and uneventful night, so to speak.

But a little after 1 am, the radio keyed up, and the dispatchers called out, "9271, 9211, 9241, 9281 a 10-10 in progress involving numerous subjects."

Knowing my ten codes well enough, I knew that the call was for a "fight in progress" and in this case, it involved several subjects to which Greg let out, "shit-head gangs."

After the dispatchers called all the area units, Greg turned on the overhead emergency lights, and I held onto the "oh-shit bar" on the passenger's side of the squad, and we took off to the call.

You know, the "oh-shit bar" being that factory-installed bar in the window frame of your car, that your passenger grips onto when you drive like a maniac? Yes, that bar and I hung on to it as it was very much needed.

Let me paint the picture for you, having never gone "code" at this point in my life and assuming that you have never gone code either. We discussed it in the academy, but never executed or trained it.

Code is what we call going "lights and sirens" to a call. In this case, it was the overhead emergency red and blue lights only and no siren.

Now, if you are asking yourself, "why no siren?" it's because of the tactics that are necessary for the environment at the time. It was after 1 am, and the streets had very little traffic, so there was no need to use an audible emergency indicator to part the traffic for a squad to navigate.

The call was also a high priority, and the noise carries in the night. You don't want your offenders knowing you're coming. We didn't want them running, as we'd rather be able to investigate as required.

Now, if you are new to driving code, especially at night, you need to know that a first-time experience will always have you feeling like a little kid at Christmas. Except instead of Santa coming…YOU are.

The speed, the excitement, the streets lit up from the reflection of the red and blue strobes casting all over everything, and all the houses, buildings, trees all lit up as you fly by…it's an adrenaline dump, to say the least.

Then looking ahead as you travel west on the main street of the town and see another squad car speeding straight towards you east with their lights on and seeing/feeling it as he cuts north right before you do, only to look in your rearview mirror to see yet another lit up squad right behind you from the south as you all form a wolf pack running forward; "Damn" was all I could think.

It was at that moment that I realized I was part of a brotherhood. It was a very powerful moment and rite of passage traveling from a citizen to a police officer who was now part of the process in what we do to keep people safe. It just happens to be that some of those things we have the responsibility of doing are kind of awesome.

We all pulled left into the subdivision where the fight was dispatched to be taking place. All four of our squad cars were pulling in "blacked out." This again being a tactic where all of our lights, including our headlights, were turned off as we slowly approached the scene as to not alert the bad guys that we were coming. The only annoying thing I remember to this day is that those damn Ford Crown Victoria's had brakes that squealed no matter how slow you went.

The moment we got out of our cars, I saw three guys running from the scene, a state trooper running after them and two other squads from the neighboring town pulling up. It was a lot to process, but I remember being proud I didn't freeze up, instead went right into action mode, running towards the trooper.

The state trooper had later told us that he heard the call on the radio and when he got in the area, he saw ten to fifteen subjects all fighting in the alleyway, hence why he pulled in to help us on our call.

So, five of us ran after the subjects who were running.

To paint the picture better for you, I was running next to and a little behind Greg (my FTO) as to not fall out of his sight. He was responsible for me, and his orders from the start of the shift were to not leave his side unless he ordered.

I still didn't know the area at all, there were barely any streetlights to light the dark and I had no clue who the hell we were running after. And remember what I said about what the academy left me thinking, that "everyone wants to kill me."

Now, let me back up a bit and give you a little insight into my past. I am no stranger to physical violence. I grew up as a competitive wrestler and worked in a 4 am bar for years before becoming a cop. Am I or was I a violent man? No. But do I shy away from a person who is violent towards me? Not a chance in hell. I am a very competitive, "Type A" personality and a shorter man, to boot, who has no problem walking up to any challenge and staring it in the eye. I do not like violence, but I am damn good at it.

And it takes a person with that mentality to be a police officer, whether you understand this or not. I am not asking if you agree or not, but I am telling you that you need to accept this and that part of the culture of the police is to have men and women who have the desire to run towards the danger in order to keep you safe.

The only way to defeat violence is with superior violence. Accept it.

That said, it wasn't the fight in progress that concerned me. It wasn't the dark streets or the unknown. It was the possibility that I could screw up and get in trouble somehow that was gnawing at me as we searched for these guys.

After circling the complex, we met up with another officer who was standing at the front door of an apartment. These were all first-level units, four units altogether, which lined up to form little alleys in which we first saw the subjects running from.

Officer Sharon was standing at the front porch of this house, waving us over to her. Greg and I walked over, and she said, "I saw one of them run in here."

I stood behind her, probably about ten feet back and to the right of her so that if the door opened, I had a line of sight on the inside. Greg was about ten feet behind me, most likely observing what I, the probationary officer, was going to do but still in a safe position to bail me out if I needed help.

So, standing there, in the dark and the summer heat, trying to catch my breath after running around this building to chase these unknown gang members, I watched as Officer Sharon started knocking on the door. And by "knocking" I mean that she grabbed the doorknob with her right hand and started to kick the bottom of the door with her right boot in an attempt to wake up the whole fucking neighborhood.

I was stunned.

This was not a tactic I had learned in the academy, and it was down-right rude as hell. But, I will admit that it has been added to my arsenal of tools over the years when need be. At the time, however, I was very surprised at how police "handle" things at times. And this is the very disconnect between the public and the police which must be linked through education.

So, there we were…all waiting for the door to open and bad guys to just offer themselves up to the police and say, "Yeah…we fought. You can arrest us now."

But instead, a good sixty seconds had gone by, and Officer Terry joins us on scene. And as he walks over to us saying, "I searched over there and didn't see anyone…" he stops dead in his tracks and points to the bushes that are right next to my right leg and says, "There!"

And I look over and down to my right side, and there, two feet from me, laying in the bushes (which were only about one foot high) was the guy who we later learned had caused the fight.

My First Night On Patrol

He had been laying there the whole time that we searched, the whole time that we talked, the whole time that I stood by right next to him.

To make matters worse, he was wearing a bright orange shirt that stood out, even in the night sky…and I still didn't see him.

My heart POUNDED.

Having the academy training kick in (not the physical tactics which were crap but the mentality that he was going to kill me) I jumped on him, put his hands behind his back in and handcuffed him in his bright orange shirt that was pretty much screaming, "Hey, new guy…I've been right here the whole time."

Mind racing, wondering if I was going to get killed like they had taught us in the academy, I was more terrified and worried about Greg documenting in my FTO file that I didn't notice the guy.

And the whole time I was still trying to process the necessary tactics of the door kicking and even the embarrassment of Officer Terry having to point out where this guy was, I did the perp-escort back to my squad with Mr. Orange. My mind was all over the place.

Greg opened the rear door of our squad, I put him inside, shut the door, and I felt my ears fill up with cotton.

I stood there for a second, and things got real quiet for some reason. I mean, I felt as if I had a severe head cold that came on out of nowhere. I felt the pressure swell up in my face, nose, ears…

My vision trailed off to my right, and my left arm braced against the trunk of the squad car, but I couldn't feel it. I couldn't feel either the trunk or my arm.

I looked at Greg, said, "Hey Greg…" And that was it.

The next thing I remember, I was looking at a pair of hands on my chest, opening the buttons of my shirt. I heard the sound of Velcro being ripped apart and felt it easier to breathe. It was dark. My back was braced against something, I looked, it was the building. Why was I sitting? Who was this guy pawing at me?

I didn't know this guy. He didn't have a gun belt on, but he had a shield on his shirt. Was he a cop from another town who had come by to help without finishing getting dressed? Was he a desk supervisor that I was getting in trouble with? Were they firing me? What the fuck was happening?

And then I saw it.... The big red rig and its glorious flashing red lights.

Fuck.

He was a paramedic, and I had fainted.

I was completely out for several minutes. I was out for enough time for Greg to radio dispatch and request rescue and for rescue to get up in the middle of the night and head over to us…that's a LONG time.

What they had said (which was no comfort to my well-bruised ego) was that they felt I was dehydrated, my vest and duty belt was too tightly secured, I was overheated, and I had an adrenaline dump. All of these factors contributed to me fainting on my very first night of patrol.

I literally passed out for several minutes after a fight in progress call.

The sergeant came on the scene, and I watched him talk to Greg, obviously about me as they both looked at me as I was getting up and dressed. I was beyond paranoid about being sent home and or fired on the spot.

But luckily for the rest of the night, I was told I wasn't allowed to get out of the car. And for the rest of the night, I wondered if I was going to have a job the next day. It was a long night.

And then it hit me…. The academy didn't teach me any of this. It didn't teach me how to doubt myself or how to overcome that doubt.

I never learned that you could have an ego as big as mine, but an event like this, surrounded by the people you want to make a good impression on, would leave you spending hours wondering if they doubted your ability to have their backs or worse if you

My First Night On Patrol

doubted your own.

I wondered if any residents saw. Did they see me pass out and would they call the department in the morning asking for my dismissal? Thank God this was before cell-phone cameras.

I spent the rest of the night drowning in doubt on not only if I had made the right decision in becoming a cop, but if I was even qualified in the first place.

We finished up the night, and I drove home, still drowning. I walked in the front door, crawled into bed with the girl I was dating at the time and said nothing as she woke up enough to ask, "How was your first night?"

The academy didn't prepare me enough on how to deal with the embarrassment and your significant other. It didn't teach me how to shelve pride and talk to her, nor did it teach me the damage that not talking to her would later do. That is an entire book itself for another time; how to put your relationship above all when you are a cop.

So, instead, I ignored her question and went to sleep.

I woke up that afternoon, got dressed, and drove back to work for the next shift.

Worried as all hell about what the guys on afternoons would think after they heard what happen to me in passing from day shift roll call, I walked right into midnight's roll call, sat down and did the only thing I knew how to do.

I walked in, sat down, and said, "You guys hear about that pussy who passed out last night?"

And with that, the squad room burst into laughter.

I knew I had told them all that they needed to know about me and that I was there to stay. I told myself with confidence, "You own this now and you make this your world. You are not going to fail."

Fifteen years later and I still refuse to bow down to my drowning doubts no matter how hard they try to pour through the cracks. The moments come and go much quicker now and with far less questioning, however like any self-demons, they are always around.

No, the academy never taught me how to deal with self-doubt or how to deal with pride issues. More so, the academy never taught me the dynamics of the job of a police officer or the perpetual price we have to pay while being one.

That night was the beginning of the end of my relationship and the destruction of every single other one I have been in since, at my hand. And I will talk about that later on.

Neither the academy nor life's maturity had given me that lesson yet about how to curb my ego and pride. And in the end, it was a costly lesson that I still have not yet learned.

Chapter Nine

A GOOD COP BUT ONLY HUMAN

I was a good cop.

Years had passed, I serviced tons of calls that I could go on and on about, learned even more life lessons, but I had become a good cop, nonetheless.

I had used my already damn-good people skills to gain the respect of the public and those I worked with. I had experienced the adrenaline of the job enough times to not be overwhelmed or impressed by it and had become what we call "seasoned." I also had seen heartache too many times by this point and had my fill of that ten times over.

I was a cop. Period. I did my job day in and day out loved it and had so many days where I walked away saying, "Man, the academy didn't teach me about this."

Being a cop is a constant education in becoming the man or woman you are supposed to be. And you never graduate from this school, but you always have to pay tuition.

There are no student loans you can apply for and no scholarships either. What there is, though, is compounding interest that starts the moment you swear the oath to your city, state and country.

The debt is heavy, and the tuition is constantly increasing, too. You make payments in doubt, tears, anger, confusion, sleepless nights, and wasted days. You sign yourself up for a new semester of classes that teach you about deception and the evils of man against his neighbor; classes that teach you about the horrors of crimes against the elderly, children, animals and those unable to protect themselves.

You attend lectures on feeling what's right in your gut but having to follow orders that seem to contradict it. You find yourself walking out of the classroom wondering not only if you had learned something, but why the lesson was necessary in the first place.

If I had a brick for every time, I walked out of a house, scene or a call and asked myself, "Was what I just saw not only real but necessary for me to see in the first place?" I could have built myself the biggest, strongest wall that could have shielded me from all of this stuff in the first place.

When you become a cop, you lose who you were and wanted to be and become who you were meant to be.

I wish the academy would have taught me about this.

*****

GANG HOUSE SHOOTING

MIKE TOOK A KNEE…He supported his shot with his knee braced position, took aim, and fired one round into the pitbull…. Mike hit the dog and then the damn thing vanished.

Ok, so we had gotten the call that a neighbor had concerns that the vacant house next to his was becoming a squat house.

He called anonymously and just requested that police investigate.

It was around 1630 hrs. on a very warm Saturday afternoon and in the middle of summer. I recall lots of people being out, washing cars, riding bikes in the street, kids playing. It was a very nice summer afternoon.

When I was called for backup, I was the third car on the scene. I was told to park a few houses down and to approach to the rear entrance. I met with Mike and Tim, who had already gathered intelligence on what was happening, and Wayne was in the front of the house, watching the main entrance.

From what I was told, there were several gang members in this house. They had broken in and were using it for drug activity and such. We had enough evidence to do a premise check and secure the house. Mike was going to support Wayne in the front while Tim and I gained access through the rear.

There was a small broken window in the frame of the door, which was how people were gaining access by sliding their arm in and opening the lock from the inside, so I did the same.

I cracked the door open for Tim to gain a tactical visual before entering, pulled it a bit more and BOOM!

We were met by the deep, thunderous barking of a 90 lb. brown and white pit bull on the other side of the door.

That thing barked like a savage! I swear that if we had entered one foot in, it would have dragged us in and ripped us apart.

So, I slammed the door shut and alerted Mike and Wayne over the air, about what was happening on our side. Mike acknowledged that he was coming over.

While we waited for Mike, I could hear a lot of hurried talking and loud footsteps coming from the inside, in between the dog's paused barking. I knew that there were several subjects inside.

Mike met up with us, and we attempted the door again, this time, with me shooting a stream of pepper spray inside through the broken access window, at the dog. It did control it a little bit in that the dog backed off and ran up the stairs, allowing us to gain entry.

I was the third in, behind Mike and Tim.

I pulled my Taser and lit the red dot on the pit bull, which was doing exactly the job it was trained for, holding the middle of the staircase.

We heard yelling at this point from the people upstairs. We announced, "Police, police, show us your hands!" but got no response.

That dog was ready to kill us. He was guarding his owners, the gang members, and protecting them from us. And as I took aim, I heard the first bang.

Mike took the shot from the kneeling position. He hit the pit bull, and it ran up and off to the right, disappearing. (Understand the danger of using a Taser on a dog, the Taser being deactivated and the dog running off and attacking someone else. This is a main reason why NOT to use a Taser on a dog before you get upset reading further.)

We tactically made our way up the stairs, announcing our presence and giving orders, cleared the room to the left, cleared the room to our right, guns at the ready, and…nothing.

Every room was empty. And we looked at each other like confused jackasses.

"They're running north!" we heard Wayne over the air.

Yes, all four gang members AND the shot pit bull were running from the scene. They had all jumped out the second-story window, onto some bushes and took off. The loyal dog followed suit.

So, we gave pursuit.

Now, what you have to refer back to was the warm, summer afternoon with tons of people outside. People who now heard a barking pit bull, shouting police, a gunshot, and fleeing gang members. It looked like a parade outside on both sides of the street.

Exiting the house and seeing them run, I started to pursue the gang.

I took off full steam and got about 15 feet before I heard Mike scream my name. "DOMINICK!"

I turned and looked over my left shoulder and saw that damn pitbull running right toward me! He had a round in his right shoulder, had jumped out a second-story window, fallen to the ground and STILL wanted a piece of me. I froze.

Again, let me paint the scene:

Hot summer afternoon. People all over. Gang members running from a crime scene. And a huge dog, shot, angry and coming right for me.

BANG!

I looked and saw Mike, fifteen feet away from me, fire another round into the dog, who was less than five feet from me. The pit stopped…and turned towards Mike, then ran at him.

This was crap you couldn't make up in an action film. Two rounds and the dog charged him. BANG!

Mike fired a third, hit the pit…. AND IT KEPT FUCKING COMING.

The fourth round did the job, and the threat was eliminated.

Now, understand this, I am a dog lover and there is much I can say about this, and even more I can say about the necessary tactics that were used. So, don't think me heartless on this. That day sucked, but we had a job that needed to be done.

I remember the adrenaline dump kicking in. The fact that a dog had tried to attack me twice, the running after suspects, the shooting of a pistol on the street so close to me, it was a lot of stress for me to take in when she walked up to me.

All I remember is this flip-flop being shaken in my face and her screaming, "You fucking stupid cops!"

I had no idea who that woman was or what her problem was. We were there to safeguard property that was being tagged with graffiti and used to sell and do drugs and yet the people who flooded the streets that day saw us as the bad guys because we shot the dog of the gang that was doing what they trained it to do. At that point, the dog was an abused pet that was used for a specific purpose, and those gang members had caused this. But try justifying that to people who only had a fraction of the information on the scene.

After she shook that shoe in my face for the third time, I

remember slightly losing my cool, grabbing her by the arm and walking her down the street while saying, "You'd be best to shut the fuck up and get into your house please."

Could I have arrested her? Yes, for assault. Did I have to physically remove her from the scene? Yes, she was obstructing a police investigation.

Did I have to speak to her like that? No, but I am human.

So many calls like that over the years, so many life lessons learned. The four gang members were caught, charge, and released.

Hours later, after processing, issuing court dates, taking bond, and letting them go, not one of them asked about their dog.

PARENTAL GUIDANCE NEEDED

Look, this story is beyond insensitive. It's not even remotely "PC" nor is it professional for me to talk about.

But, it happened, and it happens all the time where officers service calls like this and leave laughing their asses off because of one reason…it's real life.

The academy doesn't teach you about the awkward things you'll see that will have you busting a gut, laughing over, then telling and re-telling the story over and over at every roll call, party, family gathering and book you choose to write.

Again, disclaimer:

This was absolutely a true story (as these all are) and I serviced it with complete dignity and respect. But the moment I got in my squad, I completely lost my shit and roared laughing.

Was it appropriate? Nope.

Was it professional? Nope.

Am I a human being who experiences life and its moments? Hell yes! So, let me tell the story, judge me all you want, but know that I did and still do my job with all the respect and compassion that you expect me to, daily.

A Good Cop But Only Human

*****

The service call was a "citizen assist." Apparently, a parent needed help with their child. We get these all the time, and mostly they are for out of control kids under 10 years old or disrespectful teens that parents are afraid to discipline.

This, in my opinion, happens way too often. Parents need to parent and not involve the police or the interference of child services (but I will cover this in the near future).

Regardless, the call came out, and I went.

When I pulled up to the house, I was met by a small man who was the complainant. He wasn't small in size, however in presence. He looked meek, so to speak.

He was thin and a little taller than me. He wore glasses, had a beard, he was well-groomed and looked as if he was well educated regarding how he dressed if that makes sense. His clothing was neat, earthy tones and colors, and his handshake was soft.

I introduced myself and asked how I could help him, wondering how the heck this man could have a problem with his child, as he looked as if he ran an orderly household.

Then he spoke, and I could tell he was deaf.

Having a little sign language in my background, we spoke in both sign and spoken word.

He explained to me that he had an issue with his 14-year-old son. He told me that he wanted help with trying to figure out how to deal with it. His son was standing off in the background, and I didn't see any signs off the bat that this kid was a problem.

He was a very calm and polite guy, he was pretty cool actually, and again I couldn't figure out why I was standing there in the front yard with him.

Even when his son walked up to us after I called him over, I still couldn't figure out why the hell the police were called in the first place.

This kid looked "normal" and completely not in need of police intervention, let alone discipline, as he had absolutely no attitude with me or his dad, whatsoever. This kid, just like his dad, was well-groomed and put together with pride. He was not at all like what we were used to dealing with as far as "out of control teens."

Again, that's what we usually were called to help with.

It was a complete mystery to me, why I was called there. I looked at the kid and asked, "What issue can I help you and your dad with?"

And then it happened…

"THIS!!!" the meek, well-put-together and groomed man shouted.

He pulled out something from behind his back that he apparently had in his back pants pocket.

At first, due to training and the fear of being killed from the academy, I thought it was a weapon he pulled out. But as he continued to yell, I noticed it was just a rolled-up magazine.

He was yelling and yelling while waving all around in the air. And me, associating this as best I could, with what limited exposure that I had in this situation, kept thinking, "Man, this is going to be the most interesting answer I have to a call, ever."

You have to picture yourself standing on the front lawn of a person's house at 6 pm in the summer. The sky is still lit, and the neighbors are watching you there on the lawn with him and his teenaged son.

The yelling starts, and you look to the kid and see his eyes rolling in his head at his father and still, during all of this, you are trying to process, "Why the hell am I here?"

And then it happened…the father opened up the magazine. And I lost it on the inside.

But let me tell you, boy, I held myself together with amazing stoicism, professionalism and poise.

The dad unrolled the magazine, and there it was, in all its glory…two well-oiled muscle men, wrapping their arms around each other…NAKED.

Dad had found a gay porno magazine in his son's bedroom

A Good Cop But Only Human

and apparently the way he wanted to deal with it was to call the police.

He was waving it in my face, shouting, "What is this!? Do something!? He can't have this!?"

I was completely untrained for this, and the only defense mechanism I had was to laugh…but I couldn't, yet.

Now, it wasn't insensitive or judgmental laughter that I was holding back, but "Here's another day on the job" laughter.

I just remember trying to calm the man down and try to shield him from his neighbors seeing his business, but he wanted none of that.

I tried to explain, over and over, that this was not a police matter at all and that he needed to take this inside with his son. All the while, the son just looked at me as if to say, "Good luck, dude, this is what we call 'Friday night.'"

And with that, I spend another fifteen minutes with the meek little man screaming on the front lawn that his son had gay pornography in his bedroom and that he wanted it seized for police evidence, for a reason that he couldn't come up with.

"Take it! Take this!" he kept screaming.

Meek, well-groomed and educated, dancing around, with the heavy-duty magazine; pages making that flapping noise created while he whipped it around in the air. This gentleman had used 911 to create a moment in my life, that today, I still have no idea how to handle.

Again, the academy did not tell me the reality of when compassion for a problem becomes your reference for humor and that the only way to purge yourself is to sit in your squad car, close the door and laugh your ass off at what you had no clue just happened.

Chapter Ten

THE POWER OF GOD

THE DEAFENING SNOW
In all my years, it was probably the only time I ever remember being truly afraid on the job.

It was 2 am in the morning, and I had no intention of driving my squad anywhere due to all of the falling late February snow, the roads were horrible. Our squad cars were all rear-wheel drive, and it made for crap navigation in this weather, so I just sat in my car and read a book.

It was a very quiet night. It was an early Tuesday morning with not one call to any of our departments.

I work in an area where one central dispatch center manages the radio traffic for 5 agencies. All of our towns have the same type of calls with the same public service and criminal elements. We are all very familiar with each other's problems and help each other out from time to time.

I remember sitting in the squad, reading a book and watching out the window every so often to see the large, beautiful flakes of snow that were falling like feathers from the sky. The car dealership that I was sitting across from had these huge display lights that lit up their inventory, but tonight they lit the night sky and made the town truly into a winter wonderland.

Quiet…that's what I remember for the most part, how deafening quiet it was.

"9211, assist rescue. Child not breathing," I heard the dispatcher state. This was not a call for my town, rather it was a neighboring town, so I continued to read, but listened none the less.

"9211, go ahead," I heard the unit respond.

"9211, assist rescue, 1212 Burke St., for an infant not breathing," the dispatcher calmly stated…and then I looked up from my book and saw that I was sitting directly across from Burke St.

"9311, I am right around the corner and can respond," I stated. I put down my book, turned on my overhead emergency lights, and drove. This isn't really protocol or policy, to take another jurisdiction's call, however, due to the nature, it's good police work.

Here is what I remember:

I drove as fast as I could that the snow would allow me. I remember the ass end of my squad sliding all over the road. I only had two or three blocks to drive, but the call was a true emergency, and "getting there" was paramount.

I pulled up and slid about twenty feet in the snow, in front of the house, jumped out of my squad and stood looking for the entrance. It wasn't hard to find, though.

There, in the quiet of the winter-wonderland night, I actually heard the strobes of my emergency lights flashing as they alternated from red to blue and back in their chaotic pattern due to the deafening attributes of the snow.

I remember truly hearing the sound of the strobes and being amazed that it was so damn quiet out that I could. I even heard them over her screams.

It was easy to find the door I was supposed to go into…she was collapsed in the doorway, moaning and wailing. Half in and half out, her body was on the floor, reaching into the night as if to take someone's hand who wasn't even standing in front of her. So, I ran to her.

The snow was up to my knees as I ran through their front

yard. As I got to the front steps, he pulled up in his giant truck, equipped with a plow, onto their driveway and jumped out.

The plow driver was young, about my age. He was clearly working that evening as plows were out everywhere. What I learned, later on, was that he was the husband of the woman lying in the doorway, wailing in pain, and reaching out. She was reaching out to him. I learned later that she called him first, before calling 911 and she saw him approaching as I was running to the house.

He and I both got to her at the same time.

"Where?" I asked. That's all I remember saying, well, yelling really…"WHERE?"

Unable to speak, she just pointed upstairs. I looked at him to lead me. His eyes were huge and filled with an almost rage of confusion. He only knew to come home, he had no idea why.

I followed him as we both sprinted up the stairs, made a quick left and then an immediate first right into what was a child's room. I saw a crib…I ran to it.

There he was, laying on his back, in a dark blue "onesie" pajamas. Knowing full well that I was liable for anything that I would do, from that moment on, I was careful and cautious… but he was a baby, and I needed to act, regardless. Again, more of what the academy doesn't teach, liability vs. "Do your damn job."

I placed my hand on his chest and rubbed a little to stimulate him…no reaction.

The man was on my left, leaning on the crib, alternating his looks of confusion between me and the baby, his son.

I tried again, calling out, "Hey…baby…hey…" …again, no response.

I holstered my flashlight in its keeper, reached down into the crib and took my left hand to secure it under the child's head, back and butt so I could pick him up and try to get a cry out of him. I remember how absolutely incredible it is how time slows down in moments that we wish it would speed up and vice versa. It seemed to take forever to turn him over.

I can clearly recall how I locked eyes with the man and how his look turned from confused to desperate as I brought his son up to my face to try to feel breath against my skin…and I also recall how it felt when I felt the cold radiating from the baby's face…his blue face.

In the dimly lit room, I saw that the child's face was blue. I recall how I felt the rigid body of the infant and how the normal heaviness and "dead weight" of a sleeping child was now substituted for a stiff doll in my arms.

I had never felt a lifeless child before…I had no comparison to process the sensation I was feeling and only knew that whatever I was holding did not feel "right" in my arms.

I knew the baby was dead.

There in that cold, quiet, winter wonderland night, all I thought in that specific moment was, "Babies aren't supposed to feel like this." And I slowly returned the child to where I had picked him up. I was in horror, shock, repulsion, and asked God, "Why did you just do this to me?" I was nothing but selfish at that moment, wishing that I hadn't felt or seen what I just did. I wanted it taken away. For at that moment, it wasn't a baby I just held, and it wasn't his father who was standing next to me. It was a burden I didn't ask for and a man who was looking to me for answers that I would never have. Once again leaving me to ask why the academy never told me there will be moments of selfishness that come over us in order to protect the little humanity we have left from this job.

"Dispatch, 9311…I need rescue to step it up, and we need a shift commander here," I called out over the air, knowing full well that everyone listening knew exactly what was going on and it would get others to come to my aid. I needed them. At that moment, I felt utterly alone and unsure of myself…I was unable to associate what was going on.

I pulled the mic away from my mouth and looked at the father of the child…he looked at me and asked, "Why are you stopping? Do more! What are you doing?!"

"Sir..." I said, no, I implored, "please...rescue is on their way." And I looked down, away from him.

Disbelief is what I think came over him. It was only one or two seconds, but at that moment, I saw the epitome of helplessness in another human being...I had never seen that look before. Then fear came...my fear.

We can go back to what I said earlier about me never backing down from any threat, but this man scared me enough to make me want to run like hell from him.

This man, just about my age and my size, transformed into the physical persona of confusion, pain, rage, and initial stage of loss, and in his state, he completely destroyed the room.

I watched this little man pick up and throw the dresser that was loaded with clothes as he wailed in agony.

I saw as he took both his fists over his head, smash them into the closet doors and then drag them down it, splintering the wood in rage...and then he turned to me. His eyes were welled with tears and red with rage. I was truly terrified. I knew that if he wanted to, at that moment, he could have killed me. That was one of the only times in my life I remember taking a step back from a threat in fear and putting my hand on my gun.

But then she saved me. In all the chaos, confusion, yelling and rage, the mother of the child managed to drag herself up the stairs and into the doorway, where she collapsed and continued her cries of pain. He looked at her and then looked at me...I saw the helpless confusion return to his face...the rage was gone.

All I did was point to her and pray that he read the words in my eyes that I couldn't speak..."Sir...I am sorry. I don't even know what to say. I have no children, and I cannot begin to try to feel what you are going through. But...I am very afraid of you at this moment. I fear that your love for your son has driven you to a rage that would scare the devil himself and I am submitting to you, in your own house, after you entrusted me to save your child...I failed you...please forgive me and hold your wife."

He went to her and collapsed alongside her and together,

they stayed until the tears turned in to slow breathing with gasps for air in between. Looking almost drugged and lost, they remained motionless and still, with eyes searching for answers from men like me who had none.

Throughout the night, the room filled with cops, paramedics, our chaplain, and eventually the coroner.

They carried the little baby way in a little apparatus for children. The whole time, which was hours, all of us stood in complete silence…just as deafening as the falling snow.

I know God was there that night. I do not know what His Will was in that moment, nor, in all these years past, do I think I have a better idea what it was. But I can still look back and know that in the middle of the chaos and the quiet, He was there, right next to all of us.

I don't hate that night, nor am I distraught about it, as it has become a part of me. It is just as much a part of me as how the joy over the birth of my niece was. I was there that night, I held a dead infant in my arms, and even today, I have no words to convey how I can still feel the unnatural feeling of a cold child who didn't laugh or cry or wake up in my arms allowing for a happy ending…

Once again, never a lesson I learned in the academy, rather it was on the job training that taught me that the whole time I was there, he was sleeping in God's arms.

THE VIRGIN MARY

The dispatcher called over the air, "9211, the other units request you to expedite."

For all, you "non-police personnel," that translates into, "hurry the hell up." It also means when you hear that, your hands start to shake a little, your foot hits the gas EXTRA hard, and you get the most intense adrenaline dump there is.

Your vision becomes narrowed and focused (called tunnel vision), and you drive aggressively, while as safe as you can. You are part of the cavalry.

When you hear your dispatcher telling you to hurry up, you know you are needed by someone who doesn't normally need anyone…another Cop. That concept is both honorable and humbling at the same time. It's family, and you are emotionally invested.

The information I had, on the way to the call as a back-up officer, was that the officers from the town that bordered ours were on a call where a subject was outside, in his backyard and had threatened to commit suicide.

Based on the radio traffic I had heard, being the background sounds, as the officers keyed up on the mic and including the tones in their voices, I could tell that the subject they were dealing with was being combative…so, I stepped it up as per requested by dispatch.

I was flying down the road, behind another car, from yet another town (my old department) and we were all racing to help out.

The roads were still icy too from the snow and rain from the days before. It had warmed up a bit that day, and the sun had started to melt the February snow, but the problem was that it was now after 5 pm and the sun was no longer out to keep the streets covered in just water…they were now turning into ice sheets under the darkened sky.

Going "code" or driving lights and sirens is not as fun as you think it is, regardless of what I said earlier. After the initial excitement wears off and you understand the responsibility of it, it is stressful as hell. In my later years of law enforcement and emergency vehicle operations, I became a much more aggressive and safe driver. Contradictory terms that make complete sense if you are someone whose profession has you driving as a main responsibility.

If you are the second car in an emergency procession, you run the risk of rear-ending your partner who is navigating the traffic for the group. Mix in all the distracting responsibilities such as the computer you have for updating notes, the siren you have to operate, the radio you have to acknowledge when required to and add on driving over 70 mph in a town you do not know very well in poor weather conditions and you have a very stressful job, caked with liability and responsibility.

Now, I know some of you may read this and start to get your shorts twisted as you think, "Well I don't want my taxpayer dollars going to a bunch of cowboys who are speeding down a street they don't know very well." Just remember that you don't get to hear first-hand what it sounds like when your brothers are calling for help over the radio.

Needless to say, I may agree with you in part. However, I was glad to finally arrive on the scene so I could do my job. We can discuss armchair quarterbacking without a manual at another time.

Standard tactics for any high priority call where your target is a house, building or structure is to "blackout" your squad, turn all lights off, and park down the road, away from the address you are responding to. We talked about this before in my first night on patrol.

Seeing as myself and the other officers from my old department weren't sure where exactly we were, we parked a good block away.

Forty-plus lbs. of gear, sidewalks covered in ice and snow and officers in need of help…we ran.

Winded and breathing heavy from the run and trying not to slip and fall, we got to the house where the officers were. We were met at the front door by frantically-crying family members who were pointing to the rear door. "He's in the back!" they shouted.

All three of us ran through the house, into the kitchen and outside onto the deck in the dark.

When I got into the backyard, I was back-lit by the floodlight coming from the deck. I couldn't really see much to begin with other than the entire yard covered in snow and several figures in the yard all yelling.

I was knee-deep in snow on the deck. The deck was elevated over the backyard about three feet. There were stairs leading to the yard on the left side, with the officers being all the way to the right of the yard.

And with the snow reflecting light from the floodlight and the moon, I saw five other officers' silhouettes in the dark surrounding a tall figure that was in the middle of the yard.

"Is he armed?" I shouted as I made my way over to them in the snow, grabbing the handle of my pistol, not willing to risk my safety or the safety of the officers.

"We don't know," I heard. Not exactly an answer I wanted.

Then I heard the figure shout.

"Fuck you all! I will fight every one of you!" the man shouted.

He stood there in the snow, no jacket or shoes on, fists clenched at his sides as he paced aggressively in the snow, not backing away from us. The snow was deep, almost to his knees, but I saw him move very powerfully in it, and that's how I saw he had no shoes. The snow wasn't slowing him down like it was all of us.

"I don't care! Fuck you all! I know what you want to do to me!" he shouted.

I was informed after the call was over, that this subject had a history of violence and that each time the cops were called, the fight was usually on, resulting in him being forced into cuffs and hauled off to jail. He was a problem.

So, I went around his flank (his rear position) on his right and approached him along the fence line. I felt myself falling and had to reach out to the top of the chain-link fence for balance. Again, the snow was deep, it was dark, and I kept losing my balance as I pulled one leg out of the snow to step forward, shitty terrain to have to fight in.

Had I fallen into the snow near him, I would have been in the perfect spot for him to jump on me…and we still didn't know if he was armed or not. It was time for a different tactic.

"Hey, sir," I said, tromping knee-deep through the snow as

I walked towards him with my hands reaching out to get his attention. "Look, it's cold out, and I could really stand to go back inside and out of this shit, what about you?"

I was trying to use my people skills on him and calm him down. I had done this several times in the past and am extremely confident in my ability to talk someone down. I was confident this would work.

But confidence may have been a mistake on my part this time.

"You!" he said, raising his right hand and pointing it right at my face, "I'm fucking going right through YOU!"

Shit…

Now, remember, I've kept saying that I won't back down from anyone. This guy didn't know me, know my mindset, my skill set or the fact that he's pointing his finger at me and making that statement gave my lizard brain the green light to give him what he was asking for. I do not and will never back down. And he just told me he wanted an invite to the dance.

He was seriously a fist length away from me, and I thought for sure he was about to ask for the beast in me to come out and play. After all, he wanted to know what going right through me would be like, but he had no clue that it would only end up being a bad day for him in the end.

I inched a bit closer with my hands up and in a tactical position as to intercept any attack and unleash my own attack in response…

I had five other cops all standing watch to witness my ability as I would wreck this man who not only threatened us harm but chose me as his starting point. I was about to become the focus of not one, but three department roll call room stories for at least the next few years and be the stuff that legends are made of as they would say, "Dude, you should have seen Izzo!"…But again, God showed up first.

The man turned to me and took a short step towards me… and in the darkness of the night, the only light that was able to hit

The Power Of God

him in the darkness fell right onto his bare chest, illuminating the crucifix and scapular he was wearing around his neck.

"Hey…" I said, "I see you are wearing your scapular." That was my attack.

The man, whose fists were clenched, whose emotional rage started a fight with his family, whose face was twisted in anger at being confronted by all six of us police officers and was ready to take on all of us, stopped…placed his hand onto the scapular, raised it for me to see and he let it all go.

"You know this? You know the Virgin Mary?" he asked, as he took the scapular in his hand and pulled it away from his chest for me to see better. His voice completely changed and softened. His posture altered as he went from standing in attack mode to almost ready to collapse in relief, dropping his shoulders and lowering his head.

"Yes," I said calmly. "I know what that means to you." And with that, I walked up to him with ease, I gently took hold of his right arm, waiting and ready for him to tense up and turn it on again to fight me for making contact, but he didn't. He was relaxed and at peace.

We placed him into handcuffs without any resistance on his part. He submitted as if he felt safe. We walked him into the house and through the front where he was secured into the back of an ambulance and driven off for evaluation.

Never does it fail to humble me…the power of God, where He brings His peace to end our wars.

I do not know what the cause of the initial 911 call was. I do not know why he was in the state of wanting to commit suicide or why he felt he could take on a small army of police officers.

Nor do I know what happened to him after he was transported to the hospital.

What I do know is that I pray before and after every tour. "God…let me do my job the way you want me to. Keep me and everyone in my care safe." Again, not forcing my faith down your throat, but it's what I do. And I am proud to say that I do it.

God was there that night, as He is every night. I trusted Him to guide me, and He did.

I was ready to do it my way, handle, control, use force, and win that war if need be. But God speaks up when He wants you to listen…and I have learned to always stop and pay attention.

In a situation where men are blinded by emotions, myself more than others some of the time, I did what He asked as I did my job…I told myself, "Thy Will be done…not mine. Tell me what to do." And as always, He did.

So, what did the academy not teach me again?

Based off of a respect for everyone's right to practice their own faith, I suppose that the academy never taught me that I would get closer to God doing this job.

By no means am I pushing my faith on you, but simply sharing what I found in the academy and what you may come across yourself.

The academy talks about mental health issues, I am sure now more than ever, and the compassion we must show for these people we serve and care for. But the issue is that there is no lesson plan or manual for self-discovery and what we lean on in times of stress.

In my time at the academy, I don't recall any classroom discussions on how to debrief yourself or detach yourself from the calls you go to. But then again, that's the issue…you can't detach yourself.

Each call becomes an extension of you, weaving into the fiber of who you are growing into; both the officer you are becoming and the man or woman you are evolving into.

We never stop growing, and police work is one of the most infamous professions out there in which we are almost launched into a "grow or die" state of being…pressure-testing and problem-solving.

I had a chief once, who I really did not respect and to this day don't, who had a view of us as diamonds. And he was more right than he knew and that was the only time.

See, diamonds are forged under pressure…extreme pressure over time.

And either the coal crumbles or the diamond is formed. The same can be said for a police officer. Again, the academy never taught us that.

Chapter Eleven

A NAZI, THE DEVIL AND "WHAT THE HELL IS GOING ON?"

A REAL NAZI
The call came out as a DUI driver; calls like these were common. We always had a lot of great citizens watching over the roads in their own ways and calling 911 when other people on the road drove recklessly or seemed to be impaired.

For the most part, these calls were usually unfounded, but sometimes citizens helping us locate drunk drivers and such, proved to be a great relationship.

But this was nothing like I had ever expected it to be.

The call came over the radio as a white station wagon-type vehicle, driving all over the roadway, eastbound on Rollins.

Seeing as it was nearly 3 pm in the afternoon, the roadways were full of cars and navigating was very difficult. Again, when calls like this come out, we don't recklessly weave in and out of traffic ourselves and endanger the lives of other drivers just to find a call that a passerby or observer called in to report.

But, I found the car with some ease and followed it for just about two seconds before I saw that the caller was absolutely right for calling 911.

The car was weaving all over the roadway. In the four-lane divided Rollins Rd., the car entered oncoming lanes as well as drove onto the shoulder of its own. It did this as normally as if it was driving like this on purpose.

I activated my overhead red and blue lights and blasted my siren. No response.

The driver continued to weave in and out of its lane and all over the roadway. The odd part was that the car was seemingly only traveling at about 10 mph or less.

Constantly updating my dispatcher and wondering if I was going to be ordered to terminate this "pursuit," I moved to the outside of the driver's side of the car, at a massive birthing distance, in order to see if I could get a look at the driver.

I ran parallel to the white wagon for about fifteen seconds, at which time I saw him… a much older man was slumped over his steering wheel. He was somehow operating his car as he had his forearms and chest up against the wheel and he was somewhat pulling himself over the top of it to look over the dashboard and out into his path of travel.

I immediately notified dispatch so my command could hear that this might be a medical issue and not so much a DUI, this way I knew they would not terminate the pursuit.

I continued to travel at the driver's side of the vehicle, trying to get his attention and had no luck.

But by an act of God, his vehicle slowed to a crawl and he veered onto the shoulder of the road, idling speed was the only thing keeping the car moving.

So I sped up, t-crossed his car about twenty feet ahead of him, just in case he continued. I preferred to answer to command on why I let him stop with the use of my squad car as a barrier instead of the park that was filled with kids, which was up ahead.

I slammed my squad in park, ran out of my car and ran straight to his.

Now, this was summer, and his windows were open, so I caught a break.

A Nazi, The Devil And "what The Hell Is Going On?"

I ran up to his car, pulled a *Dukes of Hazard* and ass-slid over the hood of his car and over into the passenger side window with only my legs sticking out.

I yanked the steering wheel right so we could continue onto the shoulder and away from my squad and then slammed his shifter into park.

Yes...that part hurt as my waist hit the doorframe.

The rest of the stop was uneventful thank God. No damage was done, no one was hurt, and Rescue pulled up on the scene to evaluate the man, with no signs of anything medically wrong. We had no clue what was going on other than the fact that he was just an aging driver.

The gentleman, who was in his late eighty's, was not the most responsive person, but he was alert enough to refuse being transported to a hospital for further evaluation. So, I took him home.

He said he had his wife at home and that she would take care of him.

Sadly, I had to have his car towed as he was unfit to drive. For the most part, that is what I thought my day was going to consist of; writing a report on an old man to revoke his license. I was starting to feel like crap over it too.

I thought of this the whole ride over to his house and how I was a young man who was going to remove a privilege of his after all that he has done for our society over his own life. Who the hell was I to do this to him, right?

I drove into the unincorporated portion of our county. It was a few miles outside of our town, and none of us really ever went there. Firstly, it was outside of our patrol, second, we rarely got calls from county sheriff deputies to back them up, which always made me wonder how often they really patrolled there too.

I pulled up to his house and immediately felt the hairs on the back of my neck stand up.

The house looked just like the house of the "scary German guy" from *The Monster Squad*.

The front and side lawn was as high as my knees, with parts

of it growing even higher.

All the windows were shaded over, and the house itself looked dirty with sunken gutters and flaked paint everywhere.

Warped wood was visible, and there was no sign of any maintenance for what could have been decades.

I walked the man up to his house, called out my location over the radio, and watched him twist the knob on the front door and just walk in without any use of a key. I followed him in.

The house was nearly pitch black. Even amid the blast of sunlight in the summer afternoon, there was barely any light at all in the house, sans a single small Tiffany lamp on a table at the entrance to the living room.

And once in the house, the smell hit me and it hit me HARD. Ammonia. Urine.

I closed the door from the inside, and when I pushed it closed with the handle, I felt a film caked feeling in the palm of my hand on the knob. I felt a greasy film that was covered in dust on the knob. And when I looked at the table and lamp after my eyes had adjusted to the lack of light, I saw that this same film covered them as well.

I briefly looked around the room, scanning, just like I always did in every single place I went to. I accessed my entry points, exit points, tactical positions, etc. Just the normal habits of what I did, regardless of this old man not being any kind of threat.

And he just stood next to me, motionless, saying nothing and just staring at the floor as if being scolded.

I turned to my left and saw a display rack mounted to the wall. An open display rack filled with pistols. I thought nothing of this.

I was and still am pro-gun and had seen many display cases and racks in my time.

All the guns were caked with dust and a greasy film. I examined them all without a touch, as I did not want to disrespect this man in his own home.

And as I continued to look, raising my head from the very

A Nazi, The Devil And "what The Hell Is Going On?"

bottom of the rack to coming up midway, I just stood there in a confused state of trying to place what I was seeing.

I looked at the pistol on the second shelf from the top. I leaned in and felt my face pinch.

"Is that...is that a Luger?" I asked the man. I was absolutely certain that it was. I had never seen one in person before and only saw them in the movies when the actors who played Nazis carried them, but I was certain that this was a Luger. The old man said nothing.

And then it caught my eye...how did I not see that before?

Were my eyes not adjusted to the lighting and that's how I missed it? Was it so rare of a thing to see that I just didn't comprehend what it was? How did I not see this and what the hell was I into right now?

Out of the corner of my left eye, I was pulled back to focus on the wall that the Tiffany lamp lit up as I walked in. I felt my eyes widen, my heart start to pound, and it pull me toward it as if I wasn't in control.

There were three small framed pictures on the wall, right as you walked in the doorway, over the table and cast in the light of the lamp.

In these pictures was a young and handsome man. Dark hair, strong look. He was smiling, and he was with other men.

The black and white photos of these men were old, they were dusted over too but clearly visible...as were the SS emblems that were on the collar of their uniforms.

I leaned in closer and felt the words come out of my mouth in a whisper, "Are you...were you..."

"We had to fight for Hitler, or he would have had us killed!" a thick German-accented voice shouted at me from across the room.

I snapped to attention in time to see an old woman walking towards me with her fist shaking in the air at me, and in that moment, I knew who he was...he was a Nazi.

"You had to! You had to fight for him!" the old man's wife

told me. She seemed to plead with me in her statement. And at that moment I don't know who felt more threatened or afraid, her or me.

I did not stay long, I did not want to. And I didn't ask any questions as I did not know who else was in the house or what I had gotten myself into and I wanted to do my job and leave. Something just didn't feel right about this place, and I was alone and had no backup.

I took as much information as I could and left. I had no further need to investigate and didn't want to corner the wolf any further.

And I don't know whatever happened to them.

I did my report for our department, and I called the FBI that day and gave them all the information that I had…. They never updated me with a result of their investigation, and I never went back to that house again.

Chapter Twelve

TEARS AND GUILT

Halloween
I didn't call Gil this year.

I mean, why would I, after all, he and I haven't spoken, and he is the chief now and very busy. Plus, what's the point? Why should I bring up the past like that if it didn't hit my mind until now, anyway?

But in 2004 he was my sergeant…and I had to take a piss like there was no tomorrow.

My bladder was just as full as it was the day that woman jumped in front of the train to kill herself and I had to park my squad two blocks away just to show up to see her mangled body. I was hurting then, and I was hurting again.

I walked into the department locker room, stood at the urinal, unzipped my pants and ahhhhh.

And then it came out, "shit."

The damn dispatch tone.

The "tone" was notification for everyone who shared the frequency to stop, listen, don't talk and listen more.

"9273, 9293 hit and run, child vs. car."

That was me. And that was Gil.

I zipped up my pants and ran out the door towards my squad car. Got my keys off of my duty belt, unlocked the door, jammed myself into the seat, geared it into reverse and slammed on the breaks right before hitting Gil's Shift-Commander squad as he was speeding out of the parking lot from behind me.

We tore down the street and continued to listen to dispatch for updates. When people ask me about being a cop, I try to use parts of this story to highlight the multitasking that is involved, compounded by stress that is suppressed by training.

I tell them to think of it being Halloween. You are at the urinal emptying your bladder. You get a call of a child that was hit by a car, and you run to try to get to the scene.

You drive behind your sergeant, doing 60 mph down a street full of trick or treaters that is posted as a speed limit of 20 mph and you try not to hit them, while listening to your dispatchers for updates on a possible fleeing offending vehicle, watch for traffic, watch your computer monitor for updates, watch yourself and try not to rear-end your sergeant who's trying to navigate the streets because he's been behind the desk for so long that he's forgotten how to get around lately.

But I try not to tell them what it was like to turn into that cul-de-sac and see a mob of people standing there and waiting for you like it was a parade.

Watching and seeing the horror on all of their faces as if you were driving in slow motion and they were pointing the direction for you to go with one outstretched arm while waiving to that direction with the other.

But it wasn't slow motion. I took that turn at over 40 mph and saw four houses down that Gil had stopped his squad which forced me to slam mine to a stop so hard that the seat belt left a skin-tearing bruise on my shoulder.

I never tell them what it was like to run out of my squad towards the mob that formed what looked like a high school fight ring at the bike rack after class let out.

But what was that sound? That wasn't two grown men fighting? What was that sound? It was something that I had never heard before but would be reminded of it again years later on a cold February night when the snow fell so softly that the sound was the only thing heard that night.

Pain.

She was kneeling on her front lawn. He was cradled in her lap. He was five years old.

She was covered in his blood, and she was wailing the sound of what no human being should ever hear; the sound of a parent holding their dead child.

She didn't know it then, and neither did we, but the medical flight crew who showed up shortly after gave me that look which was accompanied by the shake of a head which told me I should have known.

I remember Gil dropping to his knees and asking her to take the child. She gave him over to Gil so fast as if to beg him to do something. And he tried. God, he tried.

I remember standing over Gil's shoulder feeling utterly helpless and only contributing by keying up my shoulder mic and ordering, "Dispatch, tell Rescue to step it up!" to which, years later dispatch told me that when they heard me say that, they just sat there, frustrated themselves, because I was giving them a request that was already in route.

Gil rocked the little boy. He tried to get him to open his eyes, "Hey! Hey! Baby, hey!" and looking back, maybe that's why I said that on that cold February night to that little 5-month-old who was dead in my arms; because I was reliving watching Gil.

Gil was now covered in this little boy's blood himself. The boy's lifeless head rocked back in Gil's cradled arms, and I saw concern, passion, sadness and helplessness come over Gil's face.

I could see that, but the bystanders could not. They saw purpose and relentless conviction to do his job. But I knew better because I was feeling it as well.

The little boy's mother continued to seek desperate help from us. But there was nothing we could do but wait for Rescue. And then she found the breath in her chest to let out her pain again. Her sadness struck my heart and started to push out against me as if pushing outward on my ribcage in an attempt to tear my chest open.

Flight showed up, the boy was airlifted, and I transported the parents to the hospital at over 110 mph down the tollway.

The piece of equipment that he was playing near was not secured. It was not a car that hit him, but a trailer that housed landscape equipment that was parked on the street.

He pulled the handle for the door and the spring that was supposed to control that door's outward falling landing onto the ground was broken.

The door fell on top of the little boy, and on Halloween, around 4 pm that Sunday, 2004, it crushed his little body and killed him.

I stayed with the family for hours in the emergency room. I am not sure why I did. I didn't have to. I think maybe I wanted to give them hope. They made their calls to their family, and they sounded hopeful. So how dare I take that from them.

The nurses came in and out of the room, looking at me, then away, never giving me any sign of confirmation but not having one was a sign in itself.

Then I watched as the parents were told their little boy had died…and left without a word.

That sound. My God that sound. I had no idea that humans were capable of creating such harmonious chaos from the pain that made a total stranger like me cry his whole way back to the department.

CPR IN THE ACADEMY VS THE STREETS

"Annie, Annie, are you OKAY!?"

You guys remember saying this in your First aid/CPR class?

Well, let me be the first to tell you that its nothing like putting your mouth over the cold plastic of the fresh alcohol swabbed doll and breathing into its mouth-hole with that smell permeating in your nose.

It's nothing like doing the chest compressions on its hollow and limbless torso, either.

It's more like this:

The cab driver had called 911 after checking the back seat of his cab and seeing that the guy had left a coat back there. He drove back to the house, and when he got out, he saw that the man wasn't breathing.

I begged to differ when I got there.

The man had apparently climbed onto the one stair at his side door, attempted to open the door, lost balance, and fell backward.

His head was in the cold mud, and his shoulders and back arched onto the single step, with his legs in the doorway…he had cut his own airway off.

He was purple, but he was breathing very shallow.

It was very cold out. It was the end of March, and there was a little snow on the ground. It was around 9 pm, and the night's sky added to the cold. It was a very awkward position to get to the guy, and it was nothing like they teach in the safety of an open classroom with flat surfaces everywhere.

There was spit, vomit and mud all over his face. Again, it was dark, and I couldn't see exactly how he was positioned other than I was damned if I did and even more damned if I did nothing… my heart was pounding.

What they don't teach you in the academy is the overwhelming sense of, "what do I do? This guy isn't lying flat like Annie, and I have no idea what I am supposed to do, legally, morally, ethically, immediately…and I am scared. I am scared to fuck up and move him, to make things worse, not move him and have him die. I am scared that I don't have the right answers, and I am a cop and supposed to all the time."

Now, this wave of questioning rushed through my head in less time than a fraction of a moment of thought, but it seemed like much longer. The only good news to this story is that the paramedics were almost immediately on the scene the same time

I was. Those guys are physics geniuses, always looking at the math of a problem and positioning and re-positioning how the human body must be altered and moved in order to be cared for.

After the man was transported, we made entry into his house to see if we could find a contact number for someone he was related to.

Rooms upon rooms indicated that this wouldn't have been the first or last time he had put himself into his own harm's way. I had never seen so many empty Icehouse Beer cans, thrown all over. Not even in a college fraternity house would there have been such an open display of alcoholism. And this man lived alone and someday, someone would have found him in a much more horrible state.

Aside from one other incident, where I had to do chest compressions on another man, who later died while sitting in an office lobby, the academy never teaches you about the guilt or anger you have at yourself over not being able to save someone. Nor does it teach about the irritation you feel when asking, yelling, ordering for those around you to help you…and they do nothing.

You're not told how your heart will race, your head will get foggy and you will feel as if you almost have to pass out from all the chest compressions and not breathing.

You're not told about how hard you actually have to compress on a person's chest. So hard that you actually think you're going to break a bone because it's winter and all the layers they have on.

CPR is nerve-racking, stressful, and completely unrewarding.

No certification teaches you to wash off the feeling of helplessness as you drive home, replaying the events of the call over and over and knowing that no matter what you did differently, the outcome would have been the same. No outcome would have been your fault, but that doesn't change the fact that you became super-human since you got that badge and no one dies on your watch.

Still waiting for the academy training to kick in that doesn't have you pull over on the side of the road and wipe the tears of guilt out of your eyes so you can resume driving.

Chapter Thirteen

YOU GIVE COPS A BAD NAME

In all my years of law enforcement, looking back, I have a massive swelling of pride and rarely have told myself, "I am disappointed in how you handled that call."

Sans one specific traffic stop.

Looking back on this call, if I could do it all over again, I would have done it completely differently.

I was on midnights and a rookie. Two months into being on my own after getting off-field training.

It was a mild night, a nice breeze, and I was on patrol. It was Friday and after midnight.

I was patrolling the area assertively and trying to work on my skills for investigative DUI stops. I was "hunting" to remove impaired drivers off the road.

It was a few hours into my tour when I was sitting on the corner of Fairfield and Lake Shore in my town when I observed a grey Jeep Cherokee exit the parking lot of the bar that was on the corner across from me. Yes, I absolutely was "poaching." As long as your driving was lawful, then I had no reason to stop you. But this guy's wasn't even close.

The driver exited the bar, traveling southbound on Fairfield, in the northbound lane. And he didn't correct himself either.

He continued to travel south in the north lane for about a

half of a block, before severely over correcting his lane usage by swerving into the southbound lane abruptly. I had my probable cause for the stop.

Upon initiating a traffic stop, I approached the vehicle and spoke with the driver who had his window rolled down.

I immediately detected a strong odor of alcoholic beverage coming from inside of the vehicle and again on his breath when he spoke to me. I observed the driver had red, bloodshot eyes, slurred speech and had difficulty holding his head straight while speaking to me.

I asked the driver to step out of the vehicle when he handed his wallet to me…. At that moment, when I saw what was inside of the wallet, I should have continued with my investigation instead of calling my sergeant over. He was a cop.

As it turns out, this was a county officer who had just left the bar, celebrating his promotion to sergeant.

On the stop, the cop was fine, as he stopped talking to me and communicated only with my sergeant, who had taken over the stop.

I was given instructions by my sergeant.

"Dominick, park his car in that lot, take the keys with you and drive him to Gurnee. His commander will meet you there, then give the keys to him."

I thought I was doing the thin blue line of brotherhood a favor. As it turns out, it was the biggest regret of my career.

The moment I put this cop in the back of my squad, to drive him to his boss, the bullshit started.

Twenty minutes of abuse in a long cop-car ride for a man who just won the get out of jail lottery.

"Fucking rookie. You're not a cop. You have no idea who I am. You'll see," and it continued the whole ride to Gurnee.

I was pissed. I felt my blood pressure pounding in my ears at every word that came out of this guy's mouth. I had not been trained in the academy or on the street yet, that the biggest pains in the asses to cops are other cops.

Long and short of the story is that there was an investigation a few weeks later. I was asked to go to county, and I was interviewed. They apologized for his behavior. He never did.

I had seen him three times since that night, and he had risen in the ranks too. Never once had he ever taken a moment to talk to me about that night or explain his side, as the benefit of impairment would have been given on my end.

So, I had to swallow that one and I vowed never again to give another cop a break like that. Harsh? Sure. But I have gotten to know several cops over the years who have abused their off duty authority and who have also used their status to screw over other cops.

Sadly I have arrested a few cops in my career and have been extremely professional with them as that is the least I could do.

But in the end, I regret not hooking that county sergeant but have gotten some sort of peace after hearing from his wife, years later, that he's a complete asshole anyway.

Be clear about this right now: other cops are not your friends. They are your family, but never your friends. You will learn that the hard way in your career at one point, trust me. They will bail on you, turn their back on you and act like they never knew you. Of these, command staff is and always will be the worst of them.

Know this now and you will have greater peace of mind.

OFF DUTY TIME

I will say this as clear as I can…DON'T BE THAT GUY.

I met my friend at a bar one night for a late dinner. I really don't drink much, but bar food is almost impossible for me to refuse.

There we were, about 2300 hrs. or 11 pm, as the bar door swung open and this guy came falling into the bar, tripping over his feet while yelling.

Several guys walked in after he did, all loud and laughing at him.

I didn't notice it for a few seconds, as to me it was just another drunk coming into a bar, but I noticed that this guy who stumbled in was handcuffed. A little confused myself about what was going on, I was having a hard time registering that he was with a group of guys, all loud juvenile types who were making asses out of themselves and he was in handcuffs with his hands behind his back.

In the process of trying to rationalize what was going on, the handcuffed guy looked right at me and yelled, "Dominick!"

I had no idea who he was, but it wasn't too far-fetched for me to be recognized as I had worked in the area for several years prior to becoming a cop.

He marched right over to me, well stumbled really, and continued to call my name, "Dominick! Dude…get me out of these will you!?"

There was something about the handcuffs that associated me to who he was…he was a cop.

And in the instance I connected the dots, I became infuriated.

He was a probationary officer from the town next to the one I worked in. Probationary, meaning that any and all screw-ups were unacceptable.

As he got to me, I took my keys out and went to use my cuff key on him. I started saying, "what the hell are you doing?" when another guy walked up to me and stopped me, "Hey, what are you doing!?"

Me, being someone who hates being challenged, looked at him, and said, "I'm a cop."

This second, loud, drunk, juvenile patron looked at me and said, "Well, yeah, I'm a cop too."

I told him to unlock the cuffs on the first guy and with a little hesitation on his part, he did.

It was a stupid, stupid display of unprofessionalism, and it pissed me off.

What's the point of this story?

I had zero issues calling the probationary officer's FTO the next day and telling her what happened. After all, she was one of my best friends.

And after finding out where the second guy worked, I called there too, seeing as one of their sergeants was a close friend too.

Needless to say, neither one of them are police officers anymore.

Am I a snitch? You bet your ass I am when it comes to this.

You are given the right and responsibility of taking away a person's freedom or life on a daily basis. Do not, I repeat, DO NOT disgrace this responsibility by making a fool of yourself and tarnishing the badge that we all wear.

No, I have no compassion for any idiot who is out at a bar and gets drunk while bragging about himself/herself being a police officer or any other setting that causes public mistrust for that fact.

We have a hard enough time showing our best in uniform that we don't need help falling apart off duty too.

Think, think again and then think it over again when it comes to your off duty actions. Am I a little self-righteous when it comes to this? Absolutely and I am unforgiving too.

Too many people would have made amazing officers who did not get hired and yet you did. Honor them and always be your best.

FIGHT IN PROGRESS/SUPER SHARON /THE CRYING 6-YEAR-OLD

She did it again…

She damn well stuck her nose where it didn't belong, just because she could.

Here's the thing about police work that they definitely don't cover in the academy…personality conflicts.

Yes, they spoke about integrity, and I agreed 100%. Like if you found out, another officer had a substance abuse problem, would you bring it to the attention of the command staff? Well, would you?

The answer had better be, "yes" for a handful of reasons, partly being because you are morally accountable for what he/she does, to represent you after you have knowledge.

But the academy didn't discuss what happens when an officer does nothing wrong by the book, per se, but is the most loathed person you all work with and there's not a damn thing you can do.

Sharon had a problem…she was 110 lbs. soaking wet but 500 lbs. of mouth.

She was infamous for saying, "go ahead and piss me off… I'll have 5 other squads here in seconds." And once the other cops cleaned up her mess (which she always had a way of starting), she'd spout off at roll call on how much of a badass she was, kicking a 6'3" and 250 lbs. man's ass because you couldn't.

Not for nothing, I lost all respect for her the night we looked for a subject, she violated their civil rights by barging into the house of his family at 3 am, tracked mud all over the house while searching from room to room for him, then after we left, she blamed me, over the air and for all to hear, on how the family was pissed at me for going in their house and getting mud all over.

She was amazing at making messes, having you clean them up, and then her taking all the credit for the positive outcome.

It should be no surprise that she was punched in the face, by an officer, from another town she worked in, due to her antics. And understand something, I do not now, nor did I then, nor will ever condone a man hitting a woman. I wasn't there, only heard rumors but also know that she liked to cause problems. So, this was no shock when I heard she had been knocked on her ass.

She was not well liked at all by us, well, me at least.

The call was a "fight in progress" at the gas station at the major intersection of our town. The call came right out at roll call, and I was dispatched along with Ofc. Terry.

Dispatch radioed that one car, "the offender," left the scene south from the location.

How we knew who was the offender and who was the victim was purely irrelevant until we did the investigation, but someone always claims to be the other.

Now, like I said before, I never back away from violence and usually give a person what they are asking for…

You want my worst, then come at me with yours. You want my respect, that's what you will always start out with until you show me less than. I loathe violence but do not shy away from it when it is needed.

That said, I have tremendous pride knowing that I can talk almost anyone into handcuffs and rarely find myself using force.

Maybe it's the look I give off, maybe it's the physical size of me as I am well built. Maybe it's the fact that my uniform is neat and tailored, maybe it's just me…but the point is that I am very compassionate and use force when it's the last option and have been this way my entire career.

Sharon, on the other hand, bragged all the time about her "resisting arrest" charge count and that she could kick anyone's ass. Basic entry-level insecurity.

Sharon wasn't dispatched to this call and unfortunately, there's no professional way of going over the air, "don't come, we don't need you" without some waves being made later. Looking back, I wish there were times where I had said that, as it would have been much easier to deal with her not there and have her complain about me calling her off of the calls I was sent to.

I was the third car on scene…

Sharon had spotted and stopped the car that had left the gas station fight about four blocks from the gas station. Terry was with her.

As I pulled up and got out of my car, I saw Sharon pointing her finger in the face of and yelling at the driver, who she had gotten out of the car and had now positioned him at the passenger side of his minivan.

I walked up, and she was just berating him left and right. I kept hearing him say, "Officer, why are you yelling at me? Don't you want to hear what happened?"

I watched as she took him by the shoulders and spun him around against the minivan, at which time he kept trying to turn to her and plead his case.

Now, understand this…

Once an officer goes "hands-on," it's a decision they had made in their head with legal justification. Remove all moral thoughts from your mind with this next part and comprehend the legality of it.

Was she legally justified in turning him around with force? YES.

Was she legally justified in using force against him as he turned back into her? YES, as that constitutes "resisting."

Once he resists, does my moral compass trump the legal aspects in that I should tell her, on the scene, "Hey…back off a bit, as I don't agree with what you are doing"? YES AND NO.

If she put a gun to his head, you bet your ass I should have stopped her. But she forcefully turned him around, causing him to fight her. Does that mean that I should have let him kick her ass because I disagreed with her tactics? Absolutely not. It is my job as a partner to get HIM safely into handcuffs and then process the scene to determine the next course of action.

It's her safety I was concerned with as well as his, and getting him into handcuffs as soon as possible so this wouldn't continue. Again, academy course training not covered on how to deal with an asshole partner.

I am going to run through the scene of what happened, from my visual and sensory perspective and tell you, right now, that I filed a complaint about it immediately after. I don't want you reading this thinking that all cops are like this or that cops don't call out one of their own. We are not like this, and we do stop bad behavior.

Upon the third time of the guy trying to turn into and face Sharon, she about had enough of his resistance and grabbed him by his left arm and ATTEMPTED to take him down to the ground. Remember, 110 lbs. of body and 500 lbs. of mouth.

Terry and I had to do the job for her. We both took an arm and did what we were trained to do, we escorted him onto the ground, and both worked to get his hands behind his back.

Yes, at this point the guy was absolutely resisting.

Was it probably attributed to his adrenaline dump from having a fight at the gas station? Sure.

Was he probably hot and frustrated and didn't know how to handle his emotions while being unjustly yelled at by Sharon? Probably.

Either way, had he just complied, things would have gone much differently.

So, there we were, Terry had his right, and I had his left, both of us had our two hands on his one arm and were pulling to get them close enough together for Sharon to handcuff him. And what does she decide to do once they are practically touching each other?

Instead of reaching for a pair of cuffs on her belt, she pulls out her pepper spray and blasts this guy right in the face, yelling, "Stop fighting with me!"

It's only after this guy, Terry and I are choking on the spray that she takes out her cuffs and secures him.

But that's not all…

After we stand him up and walk him over to the car (which took a while seeing as he was blinded with snot and tears streaming down his face), we brace him against the sliding door of the minivan, and that's when we hear it…a little girl crying.

Seems we were all too focused on the guy in the fight that we didn't take the time to hear his 6-year-old daughter who was in the back of the minivan, watching us and terrified the whole time.

She saw everything and was hysterical.

And what does Sharon do? She opens the van door, takes the kid out of her seat and takes her into her arms to comfort her while saying, "Look what you made me do in front of your daughter!"

I don't remember being ever so pissed as I was then on any call in my career.

Nothing came of my complaint.

We were both sat down together in the sergeant's office, and she was cleared of any wrong-doing. She went on for five minutes about the fact that I have no idea what it's like to have to prove myself to co-workers or how people size her up on the street.

She resigned a few years later and left law enforcement, for the better, in my opinion too.

But the academy never told us how to deal with the frustrations of having co-workers that you knew, deep in your heart, were cancer for our profession and there's nothing you could do about it. It's one of the worst feelings in the world too.

Chapter Fourteen

RACE AND SEX

RACISM
Ok, let's talk about it!

It's the single hottest topic in Law Enforcement and that will always be so. And let me clear it up right now, so you have a definitive answer for your satisfaction.

I am not going to talk about government statistics, because they will absolutely back up what I am saying, so just go Google them for yourselves. I am stating this from the perspective of a street cop, not command positions, based on my total years in law enforcement to this point.

RACISM DOES NOT EXIST.

Racism, as described and directed towards Law Enforcement/Police DOES NOT EXIST, that's right, you heard me yell it in all capital letters.

Racism's fundamental purpose and goal is the oppression, defeat and restriction of a selected race's advancement, by a collective organization.

Having said the purpose of racism, the organization accused has to have the influence and POWER to do so. "The Police" as a totality, may have the power as does ANY collective organization, but CANNOT execute the power.

Did racism exist in police work with the last fifty years? I'm 100% positive it did.

I believe it did in that selective actions from individual officers went unaccounted for and unaddressed. I believe that this type of ignorance has carried over into what the public is fed to believe still happens…and trust me, it doesn't.

So, does racism happen today?

I tell you without hesitation and complete conviction that it is IMPOSSIBLE to have a racist police organization.

The police are and have been under such a microscope these last twenty years that the ability to collectively oppress a single race is impossible.

Excluding INDIVIDUAL bias and belief, "The Police" is a collective term and accusing such a collection cannot be proven, hence why no person, activist, organization, movement, government statistic, etc. will ever be satisfied with their mission…because they know they are spitting in the wind. They incite such anger and rage, with zero outcomes other than brainwashing people to think that something is happening which is constantly being proven inaccurate by statistics alone.

Racism exists when a government allows over-crowded classrooms, with underpaid/under-assisted teachers, to rob the growth and development of children who deserve it. How many kids are left uneducated, by severely underpaid teachers who take both verbal and physical abuse daily with no help? Problems in the classrooms are blatantly apparent, and these kids are perpetuating the cycle of their demise, and it's the system's fault.

Racism exists when a government allows liquor stores to thrive in areas where the very cause of the destruction of the family structure is the substance they are selling to their community. Why is it that the most profitable businesses in poor neighborhoods are liquor stores? I heard a doctor lecture on the severe epidemic that fetal alcohol syndrome has in these children and neighborhoods, yet liquor stores, alcohol, tobacco, are found all over in the ghettos.

Racism exists when the government does not give you MORE protection against the very violence that is killing your own, by your own and refuses to acknowledge it and leaves you no answers or outlet on how to overcome.

Don't talk to me about the "militarization of the police" and expect me to see your side. "Oh, but the police look intimidating!" GOOD!!! Perhaps criminals will think twice about acting out on violent crimes.

All you have to do is compare the police look of the riots in Chicago in the 1960s and today AS WELL as compare the use of force that was applied, then tell me which you prefer.

Cops in hats and ties using their batons and police dogs on rioters, or police in "riot gear" who won't even use pepper spray on protestors who are using force against them? Wake up, people.

If you want to be protected, or at least have a sense of protection, you hang around big men of stature who scare the bully. Yes, you want your officers to look like they can handle any challenge when you call 911. And if that includes them pulling up in a tank because 50 men and women are throwing rocks and flaming bottles at your house, I doubt you'll complain about their looks.

Racism exists when a government allows all of us to believe and act as if we all are equal, when in fact, we need to embrace the fact we are not...our OPPORTUNITIES are equal. Embrace this.

I am 5'7," and 200 lbs. I am built short and stocky. Do I have the same equality as an NBA Forward or an Olympic Swimmer? Hell no. BUT, I can sure as hell try out for the team.

The same goes for my education. I am a community college drop-out and not the most book smart person out there. Do you want me operating on your child if they need surgery? I highly doubt it. But if I pushed my education to the limits and became the best heart surgeon in the world, then you'd want me.

And last time I checked, I can't carry a child in my womb for 9 months.

WE are not equal, but our opportunities are.

Racism exists when the government removes the chance to learn Faith (not religion) from our lives so that we follow the lead of men instead of having the chance to find our real worth in the promise of God's true Love.

Racism exists when hate, frustration, anger, fear and doubt live in our hearts, and we refuse to see the truth in the kindness we are given from those who truly are trying to give.

Sent forth into the battleground between truth and perception, The Police are the easiest of all to blame for racism, oppression, restriction and self-defeat...because we have allowed our community members to not only believe this lie, but we as Police Officers have stood by and allowed ourselves to be lied about. I have expressed this in my views on failing to use social media as a positive means of community policing.

Any and all races in any community, needing the compassion of The Police, is the exact same as a child who has been raised in an abusive home...they have no idea how to accept the love of a person who truly is trying to show it.

And like the loving parent who allows himself/herself to take the anger of the child upon themselves, The Police have stood by long enough, silent and patient, allowing the fear, confusion, self-doubt and pain of our communities to be taken out on us.

This is the single greatest time in the history of Law Enforcement for every single Police Officer to do what we do at the core of our oath...CARE.

Racism will always exist. For it is the self-identification of a person/group who cannot comprehend the compassion that is truly shown to them.

They cannot see the righteous truth, the lasting effect or the sacrifice of innocence by an Officer in using force that takes the life of a man, who made their own choice, in order to care for the lives of those around him...they only see their own confusion, fear and doubt and use the only word they ever have been taught to wrongfully know...racism.

Our call to action as Police is to power forward with the highest of integrity, the boldest of conviction and the most honorable of compassion to the least of those who have never experienced such a gift that is our service and protection.

This is our job.

Never in my time as an officer have I ever seen, been a part of, nor heard of any single officer or collective group of officers, involve themselves in racist activity. And this is a nationwide proud statement.

The truth will be seen one day, and the police will be exonerated for the cowardly lies thrown upon them, from those who need to place blame on a group of men and women who are clearly stronger than they are.

But for now, we will power forward through the accusations with vigilance, because we are not only stronger than you or your lies, but we use your crucible of hate to put a blinding polish on our badges, that outshine your farce.

VILLAGE OFFICIALS

Look, they are not your friends, they are not your family, they are politicians who are elected, and they are very entitled and power-hungry.

In the wake of this #MeToo movement that is being exposed all over our country, I feel an unmatched level of compulsion to finally discuss the sexual harassment and abuse I suffered at the hands of the Village of Round Lake Beach in Illinois in 2004 and 2005 while working as a Police Officer for the village.

As a man, I did not see the importance of pursuing this, as males are rarely seen as victims of sexual misconduct, especially at the hands of anyone in a supervisory position or position of power. Yet our society has become one where women can openly attack men and accuse them, without regard to their own involvement towards sexually-inappropriate behavior.

As a much younger man in 2005, I did not see how this affected me and walked away from a fight that I should have dug my heels into as a sign that the actions of those in positions of power would no longer be tolerated.

Bottom line is that I didn't have sex with a village trustee and it cost me my job. She got pissed and made sure they came after me.

I hold then Chief of Police Douglass Larsson, Mayor Richard Hill and Lt. David Hare fully accountable for the actions they allowed and failed to prevent after bringing my detailed accounts of what had happened, to their attention.

The facts are simple:

I did not engage in sexual intercourse with then Village of Round Lake Beach Trustee Gina Miosi in the summer of 2004 as per her request.

I did not entertain the sexual advances or comments of then Trustees Gina Miosi and Sue Butler in 2004. I was threatened with punishment and discipline by both Chief of Police Round Lake Beach Douglas Larsson and then Round Lake Beach village attorney in October of 2005, which led to my resignation from the village of Round Lake Beach as a police officer on November 1st, 2005.

I brought these issues up to my Command Staff, then Sgt. Gil River and Lt Dave Hare on January 17th 2005 in a department memo, after an incident involving Trustees Miosi, Butler and Mayor Richard Hill and an off duty Vernon Hills Police Officer while at the Buffalo Wild Wings, 500 E Rollins Rd, Round Lake Beach Police report number 2004-16084 in which I refused to make an arrest in which Butler and Miosi ordered me to make.

Incident 2004-16084 consisted of myself and another officer responding to 500 E Rollins Rd. for a disturbance in progress involving village officials.

Upon arrival, I made contact with Gina Miosi and Sue Butler and was ordered by Miosi to perform an arrest on a subject, later identified as an off-duty Vernon Hills police officer who had come in contact with her. The entire incident is available via the incident report, including my involvement and my making immediate request for supervisor Sgt. Gil Rivera and turning the investigation over to him.

FACTS:

July 4th, 2004. Afternoon shift 1500-2300 hrs. While on duty and on patrol, Trustees Sue Butler and Gina Miosi requested a ride from me, in my squad car, from the area of 1947 Municipal Way, Round Lake Beach, to a destination blocked off for an outside party in the Fox Chase subdivision. After exiting my squad car, Miosi requested my phone number so she could call me after my shift and have me come over to her residence alone. This was done in the presence of Butler, who stated, "Gina, he's cute but too young for you."

July 10th, 2004. Afternoon shift, 1500-2300 hrs. While on duty and on foot patrol in the area of 1947 Municipal Way, Round Lake Beach for a festival, I was standing next to officer Wayne Wilde and conducting a premise check/walk-through of the festival. While at the festival and in the presence of officer Wilde, I heard my name called, "Yoo-hoo! Dominick!" and observed Sue Butler and Gina Miosi waving at me. After waving back, Butler shouted to me, "get your clothes off right now and get in that dunk tank! I would love to see you with your shirt off!" I did not respond or comply.

November 23rd, 2004. Afternoon shift 1500-2300 hrs. I was made aware by then Sgt. Gil Rivera that Trustee Sue Butler had stated to Chief Douglas Larssen that I had been pursuing Trustee Gina Miosi in a personal manner while on duty. This information came about after the completed investigation of incident 2004-16084 in which I refused to arrest the subject who was the focus of the initial investigation.

January 16th, 2005. Fire Dept Officer Joe Couture of the Round Lake Area Fire Department stated that Trustee Gina Miosi was at a village event on January 15th, 2005 with several village officials in which Miosi stated that she would use her authority to remove me from the Village of Round Lake Beach Police Department. Couture stated he believed her statement to come from my failure to adhere to her request to arrest and failure to engage in sexual activity with Miosi.

The events and timeline were first made known to my Sgt. Gil Rivera, Lt. Dave Hare and Chief Douglas Larsson on 11/26/2004. I was advised by Larsson in his office that I was "making a big deal out of nothing" and that community members who were elected officials usually let power and authority go to their heads.

I made Sgt. Rivera, Lt. Hare and Chief Larsson fully aware of the incident via a department-issued memo on 1/17/2005 after the 1/16/2005 incident with Fire Officer Couture. After submitting the memo, I was advised by Chief Larsson that I was again, blowing things out of proportion and to drop the matter. I was subject to stress, fear for job safety and inner conflict for several months after this suggestion to drop the matter.

At the end of an all-hands meeting on 9/30/2005, I was advised to write a memo regarding the full intent of my request, as I had answered "yes" to a department questionnaire as to if I was aware of any incidents of sexual harassment within the last 360 days and that I had wanted an investigation conducted as myself being the victim.

On 10/07/2005 at 0900 hrs. I was interrogated by village officials, including then village attorney, regarding the matter. I was denied union representation, as FOP rep officer Sandy Molidor was ordered to leave the room and told, "he isn't entitled to representation."

I refused to answer any of the village's questions, fearing the unorthodox methodology of the procedure and was threatened disciplinary action by the attorney and Chief Larsson, including possible termination, for not cooperating.

I was advised I was under investigation for breaking chain of command and not notifying the village attorney first, and going to my immediate supervisor Sgt. Gil Rivera.

Upon photocopying the Round Lake Beach Police Dept policy and procedure, highlighting my correct chain of command, I returned to the conference room to find the village attorney and Gina Miosi discussing the incident in which I was the complainant against Miosi as a victim of her inappropriate sexual conduct and observed both of them laughing at the incident.

I submitted my resignation from the Round Lake Beach Police Dept to be effective November 1st, 2005 and was never given an exit interview.

*****

This is the factual account of the events that occurred while I was an active Police Officer for the Village of Round Lake Beach.

I was a candidate for the K9 program in 2005, however, suddenly removed from contention after my notification to my command staff of the incident.

I was shunned from all command, except Sgt. Rivera who had actively and continually used his position to fully investigate the incident and mentor me in a positive aspect to ensure that my continued service for the village was unaffected and remained productive.

The incident and conduct of Chief Douglas Larsson and Lt. Dave Hare toward me included minor discipline and passive-aggressive emotional attacks, which made the job impossible to continue without daily fear of discipline.

It's been thirteen years and I let it go. The daily petty behavior, threat of discipline and psychological warfare that police command is well versed in towards their officers is an epidemic in Law Enforcement. Common citizens have no idea how police command will silence officers to prevent exposure to their own misconduct.

Most all discipline in police departments towards officers is out of personality conflict and a desire to silence an officer instead of being toward actual productivity, lack of or credible warranted documenting their performance.

I removed my opinions from this and kept the timeline factual, names accurate and my account as it was back in 2005.

There is an epidemic in law enforcement and among women who attack men openly, attack their character and integrity, without being held responsible for their own actions.

I refused to stay silent any longer. Had I told a village employee to come to my house, get in a dunk take with her clothes off or threaten to use my authority to get them fired, I would have been all over the news. Hypocrisy is safe against women it seems.

You will hopefully never experience this as a man (sorry, ladies, I am aware you have your own sexual harassment issues) but keep your eyes open at all times when dealing with these politicians.

Chapter Fifteen

THE GREAT PRETENDER

Listen to me very carefully, as I am only going to say this once. And it will be written in the history of these pages as an admission of fact. I loved him like a mentor, father figure, leader and persona to strive to be like. Before I knew the truth, I had tremendous adoration, brotherly love and respect for George. But as they say, ignorance is bliss. And it is also costly. My respect and adoration of him cost me my career.

Had I known the history, had I known the backstory, I never would have shaken that man's hand nor swore that oath.

Hindsight notwithstanding, I am glad that I did, because someone had to take on the beast and that someone was me.

As of today, the summer of 2017, she is still locked up in prison, having already served nine years of a 31-year sentence which I believe with all of my heart, that she is innocent of.

She's been locked up since 2009 after she confessed to killing toddler Ben Kingan while he was under her care at the daycare center she and her sister worked at. She confessed the heinous crime to George Filenko, one of the investigating officers assigned to the case. She told Filenko, during her interrogation, that she had picked the baby up and thrown him to the ground after she grew frustrated with him. Medical evidence showed that Kingan suffered a "skull fracture" and was pronounced dead shortly after.

It takes only a Google search to cast the darkest shadow of doubt onto her conviction, as countless people have shown outrage, support, solidarity and offered medical evidence to exonerate her and to send her home to her family.

I don't want to talk about the facts of the case. I have spoken out about them and have been very public. The generalized facts are that she was interrogated for nine hours, she confessed to a crime, there was a trial, and she was convicted.

The truth is that she was bullied by a man who has no right or business in law enforcement, she was pressured into making a statement that she had killed a toddler, and there is evidence that proves all of this. I have lost countless nights of sleep over this, cried tears of anger and outrage and have personally sworn to tell her story until the truth is accepted.

With two 48 Hours, interviews and countless news stories having been done on her, having never met Melissa, this is a personal case for me. I admit that at the time of the incident, trial, and conviction, I had no personal interest in this case or Melissa. I simply didn't know her outside of a newspaper headline and brushed it off to her being just another resident of our world who did a bad thing to another human life.

In 2015, that all changed and Melissa Calusinski became one of the most important people to me that I had never met.

Late August 2015, I was standing outside of our police department as we had a makeshift roll call with the officers. I was getting ready to go on tour as I worked 1700 to 0500, and we were all just talking about the events of the day and whatnot.

Now, at this point, myself and numerous other officers were involved in a federal lawsuit with our police department and our body cameras. And that is all I can say as of writing this, the suit is still pending.

While talking with everyone, one of the officers made mention that the "Calusinski appeal is going to bring more stress on 500."

500 is a badge number. It is the badge for the Chief of Police of the Round Lake Park Police Department. That title was held by George Filenko, the man who interrogated Melissa back in 2009.

Before you go a step further reading this, yes, I am biased against this man. Yes, I have publicly called for his resignation as well as spoken out in great detail—calling to question his ability to command. I worked under and for him. I know him.

He used to have a little ritual. He liked to throw me off of my game at least twice a week.

We worked twelve-hour shifts, again and at that time, mine being 1700 to 0500.

I was Filenko's golden boy. The man gave me anything I asked for from equipment to training to any preferential treatment. This was because I made him look good, and my arrests and policing got him news coverage.

It was a good set up. I did my job, and he got news publicity. But all of that stopped the moment I discovered who he was and I backed off of my relationship with him.

When I came to Round Lake Park in December of 2013, I had been out of law enforcement for about 4 years. I had such a bad taste of LE that I swore I would never go back.

My first's department's police chief and second department's mayor were spineless and corrupt. I called them out, got a chip on my shoulder, and then resigned. I was never fired from a police department. But I was a loud-mouthed problem child.

So, I did not put two and two together that when Filenko hired me to Round Lake Park, he saw it as he was doing me a favor to get back into my beloved career.

I highly doubt that he ever thought that one day, I would see through his scam and challenge him at the highest level.

I was hired as a patrol officer on a part-time basis and sworn in full time within 6 months. I was hired for my experience, training records, and enthusiasm for policing. I know I was an asset as the responsibilities I was given were of a priority that coincides with favoritism.

I made money for the village, gave the residents a sense of security as we ruthlessly policed the garbage element out of town and was an example of what new officers should strive to be. And I have tremendous pride in all of that.

But in the late summer of 2015, all of that stopped. My heart was shattered, and the curtain was pulled back to see the wizard and the truth of the cowardly man he truly was. After the fall of 2015, I endured nearly 18 months of the same routine from Filenko…

At least once or twice a week, it was the same bullshit.

"9513, 10-19 Post 6 per 500," was always called out over the air. What that translated to was my call number, being told to head to the police department to meet with the chief.

And every single time it was the same bullshit.

He'd sit behind his desk, pretending to be looking at something online as I stood in the doorway and knocked on the frame for permission to enter.

I was always told to have a seat. And for the next hour I would listen to the same stories of his past, his friends, his connections, his self-imposed importance and then asked if I liked my job and still wanted to keep it because my productivity seemed to reflect otherwise.

And the more he did this reverse psychology tactic, the more I resented him and started to see through him. And the more I researched him. Turns out, this "Chief" and head of Lake County Major Crimes Task Force was never even a real cop.

The more I researched about Filenko, the more I learned that he has been named in numerous lawsuits, had roughly 20 police officers and civilian personnel resign abruptly while under his command, was a walk-on part-time cop who never received the proper training (all my opinion of course when you are just given a map of the town and told to call friends for help) and then schmoozed his way into the positions he achieved based on connections.

How a man in his late 40's decides to wake up and play cop one day and then is placed in charge of the most important investigations in the county and is allowed to do so, is beyond me. But the oblivious taxpayer allows it...and trust me, they paid for it. LITERALLY.

But every week, for hours, I had to sit in that office, listen to him tell me that I needed to step it up and pretend like he had something to teach me when in the end he absolutely did...he taught me how NOT to be a police officer.

At that time, I had no way of letting him know that I was shocked at the lies I was sold when he enticed me to come work for him. I had no way of relaying that I was on to him and his bullying tactics that I had then started to see mirrored in the Melissa Calusinski interrogation videos or that I was unafraid of who he was or what he thought he could do to me. Yes, he made passive-aggressive threats that all went to my lawyer, and again, I cannot disclose at this time.

As I said, I didn't know about Melissa Calusinski or her relationship to our department up until that point. But I was fully aware of Lt Charles "G.I. Joe" Gliniewicz.

*****

September 1st, 2015, I was sleeping, and my phone blew up.

It was just after 9 am, and I had gotten several calls. "Are you ok!? Are you at work!?"

That morning, that day, that hour, the world knew that Fox Lake Police Lieutenant Charles "G.I. Joe" Gliniewicz had been shot and killed by three men, and a massive police manhunt was underway.

Here is what we knew, at the time, and what the rest of the world knew.

That morning, while on his way into work for his shift, Gliniewicz stopped off at an old industrial part of Fox Lake and called out over the radio that he was going to speak with three subjects, one male black and two male whites.

Approximately six minutes after he called for back-up, he was found dead.

I called into to my Deputy Chief that morning and asked him permission to join the manhunt as this was a mere four miles from our town. I was denied and ordered to work my assigned tour that night.

Again, a Google search of the event will show the forty-eight hours after the event. The press conferences, the memorial shrines that were set up and the chaos that was surrounding the area as we all thought that cop killers were on the loose. All of us were tense and emotional.

September 7th was the day of Gliniewicz's funeral.

I worked that night, and as usual, we were all on high alert, very high strung, tense, emotional, you name it.

I was ending my day and tired, but not ready to leave as I had to hold over to drive in the funeral procession in one of our squad cars with several of our officers.

A call came out of a woman in our southernmost part of town, stating that she thought she had heard someone trying to break into her house. I fully admit I rolled my eyes after hearing the location, because not only was it miles away and a pain to get to, but it was an over 50's community and every bump in the night gets investigated there.

So, drove down there, a little irritated that I would be wasting my time on an unfounded call, and showed up to an unbelievable mess.

"9523, Joey, get down here!" I yelled over the radio.

I pulled up, pointed my spotlight onto the front lawn of the location, and saw a large shirtless man throwing large rocks and items into the house.

I exited my squad, pulled my pistol and flashlight, pointed it at the subject and began issuing orders for him to plant his face in the grass, arms spread. I only had to repeat myself twice, he complied, and I jumped on him and secured him into handcuffs.

He was big. 5'11 and at least 250 lbs. and he was on something. He had a complete crazed look in his eyes, and he wasn't making sense.

Joey pulled up lights and siren and slammed his car into park, exited the vehicle and helped me deal with the subject.

I called for rescue over the air, and we had to wait for paramedics.

Now, I want to paint a picture for you as to how I was feeling at the time.

I was emotional and stressed from the last week of wondering when we would catch the men who killed Gliniewicz. I was stressed from all of the citizens who were emotional and leaned on us for answers and support.

When I got the call to head to the woman who thought a man was breaking into her home, dispatch kept updating me of her statements. "She was scared. The man threw a large rock into her window. She thinks he's going to kill her."

The closer I got, the more that protective side of me was starting to get irritated that some wolf was threatening a member of my flock. And when I pulled up and saw that there was a legitimate and savage threat, I was pissed.

Here is what I saw in the darkness…

There was a white minivan on the driveway of the victim's house. It was running.

The sliding door was open, and all of the contents of the van were all over the driveway and front lawn. The front and rear passenger tires of the vehicle were completely blown out and torn off of the rims.

The back window was shattered out, and there was extensive damage to the whole body of the vehicle.

I walked up to the front door of the house and left Joey with the subject we had in custody. The door was dented from what looked to be boot prints, and the front picture window was shattered, with an entire mailbox, post and all, thrown right through it.

I had the caller open her garage door, and I walked in to see her, her daughter (the subject's wife) and her granddaughter all crying and shaken up. Apparently, the man was the son in law of the caller, and in his impaired rage, he wanted to get his family out of her house.

I was stressed and pissed at what he did. I remember feeling myself power walk right up to him, and the second I got there, rescue pulled up. I am glad they did as I felt my right hand raise to his throat. It wouldn't have happened though. I know I would not have allowed myself to get out of control, and Joey would have stopped me long before I would have as well.

I am just stating that it was a very emotional time that affected all of us, including how we did our jobs.

Several hours later, I finished the call, secured him into a cell, and put on my class A uniform for the funeral.

Again, you can see the YouTube videos of the procession and get an idea for yourself of what it was like. I will tell you what I felt...

I remember being hot, sweaty, and pulling at my collar about a thousand times to try to breathe better.

We were in the Antioch High School gymnasium with thousands of police officers from all over the nation. It was unbelievably emotional and so deeply full of pride to have all of our brothers and sisters together in one room to honor a fallen warrior.

We all had to sit and wait for the procession to form. It took a few hours, so we all stood around and talked with one another. A sea of dress blue uniforms, swelling pride, and sadness all filling our hearts.

Then...he walked in.

Like a stoic champion hero himself, I watched as the gym parted like the Red Sea for the man who was going to save us all and win the day... Chief George Filenko... my chief. Reflect back on my opening to this chapter where I spoke of my adoration and respect for this man. On that day, in that moment, he was my champion and I looked at him as who I wanted to be. The devil is the father of deceit and I was very much deceived, as were we all.

The Lake County Major Crimes Task Force was the investigating agency who was in charge of this manhunt. And my Chief, George Filenko, was the commander of that team.

I remember feeling unbelievably proud of him. I remember at that time looking at him as if he was a father to all of us.

He walked into the gym, right past us, didn't say a word and powered forward as if he was hunting the bad guys even at the moment. That was the only time I saw him at the funeral. And that should have been my first clue.

That day was beyond emotionally draining.

I drove our squad in a five-mile procession of police cars, all lights on and filled with proud officers. THOUSANDS of people stood outside, waiting in the heat to wish us well and honor us.

We drove a 17-mile route and at every patch of open land possible, every sidewalk, every road shoulder, stood a huge crowd of people waiting for us.

It was Fox Lake as well and every bridge we drove over, had boats, dozens of boats all filled with people, anchored and waving at us. It was amazing.

The homemade signs of support, all the people wearing blue, the children waiving, the veterans saluting, and those who recognized us and called out our names, "Izzo!"

And every single person cried out, "Thank you!"

It was an overwhelming day. I had been up for over 34 hours, and I remember being exhausted from crying my eyes out. Again, there were THOUSANDS of people all there for us, and that day, we were all one community.

It was a day of trying to heal. A day where we honored a fallen warrior and pulled together as a community to voice our pride and state our position that we are not victims and never will be…but he ruined it all.

FOUR WEEKS AFTER

In the weeks that passed, I remember little hindsight issues at the department that were clear red flags that we all were being deceived.

They moved the investigation team (LCMCTF) from the Fox Lake Police Department to the Round Lake Park Police Department, which to us as officers did not make sense. Our police department literally was a trailer while the Fox Lake PD was far more state-of-the-art. We were issued an email from Filenko advising us that any communication of what was going on inside of the department, to anyone outside of the department would result in termination and criminal charging.

There was a plaque that was honoring Gliniewicz that was secured on the squad room door for weeks, that one day suspiciously disappeared.

Filenko rarely spoke with us, was always yelling from inside the closed conference room doors and yet when he was visible in public, he had a half-smirk permanently glued on his face.

Something was just "off." It made our hairs stand up on the back of our necks and more than ever, those of us who knew Filenko, knew he was hiding something.

And don't ask me for "proof" either. I will tell you that he was hiding something the very same way you know when your children or spouse is hiding something. You just know, based on countless hours of study of them.

Filenko's ability to play poker was horrible, and I saw his tell in that office all the time when he tried to browbeat me. The name of his game was always overcompensation.

And in November of 2015, Filenko stood at a press conference and announced to the world of the truth of the investigation…that Gliniewicz had committed suicide.

Filenko went on to say that it was the worst betrayal in law enforcement that he had seen. Little did he know that his own would far surpass anything that Gliniewicz did.

But for two months, we all were highly suspect that he was hiding the truth from us. And later on, after my termination, the phone calls came in that verified we were right.

Filenko's game of deceiving the public, for his investigation, robbed us all of proper healing and pitted the nation against us as we honored someone under false pretenses.

That caused us all confusion, pain, a lack of understanding as to why and it cost the taxpayers a huge sum of money as they donated to the manhunt, paid for overtime, equipment and more.

Filenko proved that day that he was the biggest betrayal in law enforcement as he led the world on a fictitious manhunt to satisfy his own agenda and then promptly resigned from the task force shortly after. Although rumor had it that he was forced out for the mishandling of the case, compounded with Melissa's false confession and other pressing issues.

Gliniewicz's death exposed Filenko.

September 2015 to November 17th, 2016, were the longest months of my career. It was a constant state of turmoil as the pressure increased. I cannot begin to write the pressure that my co-workers or I felt, literally for the issue of the pending federal lawsuit we are plaintiffs in. But that will be a detailed part 2 of this book in time.

All I will say in closing, to set up a story for my next book is the connection between Melissa Calusinski, Gliniewicz, George Filenko and Lake County Coroner Thomas Rudd, who was arrested in February of 2017, in blatant connection of both cases.

On November 21st, 2016, I submitted a letter to Filenko, demanding his resignation.

I was terminated on December 19th, 2016.

Chapter Sixteen

THE GOOD FIGHT—
RESTORING THE BADGE

INTEGRITY IS EVERYTHING

If there is one phrase that I have used as my mantra for as long as I can recall, it's "Integrity is Everything."

And when you boil down the unessential's in life, you are left with the one thing that truly defines us when we die...our integrity.

Integrity is doing what is right, as an extension of your character, ALL THE TIME.

When it comes to the role of a police officer and his/her integrity, there is no greater measuring tool that will be used to show the officer you are.

Here is the greatest advice I can ever offer you in your career:

DO NOT LIE...EVER.

There is not one single reference, in the history of law enforcement, where I can look and say, "Yeah...if the officer had just lied in that situation, things would have gone a lot better."

Now, understand this clear distinction:

Yes, I absolutely have lied and have used lying in tactics for the purposes of investigations. I have used lies to show that I can relate to criminals and their actions when it comes to gaining confessions.

I have told criminals that I have had drug addictions in the past, told them that I had beaten the women I had dated in order to have them feel that I empathize with their domestic battery charges and I had told people that I had stolen cars for a living to offer a sense of connection for when they had stolen property... all completely untrue.

So, I have used lying as a tactic, however NEVER as a means to place my integrity in question.

And I will say this, the moment you lie, no matter how small or innocent you may think it is, you are a liar for life in my eyes.

Forget to turn in paperwork but tell your commander that you turned it in because you know you're going to turn it in, in five minutes? You're a liar. Doesn't matter how small, just be an adult whose integrity outshines the masses, as that is the men and women we are called to be.

Have I ever lied to a superior or a fellow patrol officer? NO.

And even better yet, I always know when it's time to approach a boss and let them know something could be construed as a lie if I didn't tell them first.

On my first night of solo patrol, off of FTO, I backed my squad car into a light post and caused minor cosmetic damage. I could have easily said nothing. Instead, I got a day suspension after a small investigation, but I told the sergeant on duty because it was the right thing to do.

Years into my career, I was being investigated for pulling my firearm out of its holster and displaying it while off duty in the town I lived in. I had no clue I was under investigation, and when I was pulled in the office, I told them every single detail about the incident without denial or hesitation.

I got two days for that one, but the best part of the story was when the detective who was investigating it told me, "We drove back from your town today and the whole ride back we were stressing out, hoping that you wouldn't lie about this. We would have sought termination if you had, but we knew you better."

That was the biggest compliment I had ever received to date, as I had established my integrity, which, to this day, never goes challenged. People know better.

If I screw up, I own it.

So, that's 100% your job as well. Never lie, never be talked into lying, never associate yourself with a liar. In an era where being the police is the most difficult it has ever been, in the history of being the police, now is the time where your integrity must outshine everyone else's.

Make "Integrity is Everything" your mantra as well.

LEADERSHIP

I thought I would write regarding concepts such as appearance, interaction with the public, interaction with your peers, how to balance being a "hammer" with being a "caring counselor," etc. But then it kind of hit me that all of these qualities are what I seek in a LEADER.

To me, leadership is THE single most important quality in being police officers, and it is a severely lacking quality from those who are in leadership positions. I am not sure if this is a generational thing, a command vs. patrol division thing, an apprehension to seem self-righteous amongst your peers' thing or whatnot.

I am going to address ALL the attributes to being a leader in this job from where I see their needs, within the sole context of striving to become one.

Here's the rub.... In reality, you may have just gotten out of the academy and are at day 1 in your FTO program, or you are like me, at year fifteen and still have a lot to learn, but the issue is, when a member of our flock calls 911, they haven't a clue the difference between you and me, nor do they care. They have a need and we have to meet those needs.

Being a leader, to me, is about meeting the dynamic and ever-changing needs of those who depend on us, period.

And, who depends on us? Everyone.

I depend on you. Your other brothers and sisters in blue throughout the nation depend on you to set a good example. Your command staff depends on you. The public depends on you, your family, your friends, etc. You have a lot of people who depend on you, and you must embrace the pressure of meeting their needs.

And I will tell you right now, if you cannot handle pressure, you are not cut out for this job. Being a cop is about two things: pressure testing and problem-solving.

Never mind the paperwork, the command staff, the public, and the combination of. I am talking about the emotional pressure.

Sure, there will be days that you will feel like you can do NOTHING right. Every single little call for service will annoy the very fiber of you or you may just be on stress overload from the nature of the calls themselves, but you will feel the stress of your personal failure.

You may deal with the people who call 911 because their neighbor's BBQ smoke is blowing into their yard and they want you to do something about it. Or the single mother with the attitude who didn't see why it was your business to stop her son while he was walking on the gravel shoulder of a busy street, in the middle of winter, wearing only shorts and a sweatshirt and he is only eleven years old. When she talks to your commander to complain, and you just want to shake the crap out of her and yell at her about trying to be a good mother first, you have to recognize that you are only into four hours of your shift and have the rest of the day and night to be irritated over this.

The barking dog calls, the unfounded reckless drivers, the dogs and cats who walk into a complainant's yard and do their business, the missing persons who are one hour late and come home the very second you finish all your paperwork to get them entered as missing.... I can come up with volumes of calls that I've rolled my eyes about over the years. That the moment I am dispatched over the air, I have the solution already figured out in my head. See, all of these B.S. calls for service are just not important to me.

BUT, they are beyond important to the people who need us.

I honestly can't do a damn thing about a squirrel that has made its way in some woman's home and is now causing her grief by running around in between the walls. What can I do, seriously?

What I can do is walk around the house with her, listen to her, empathize with her, spend some time with her and try to offer any solution that I can. If it is slow, I may call and ask for another officer to join me. This way, it makes her feel like a priority and that she's entitled to special attention. And guess what? She is. Everyone is. That's part of your leadership mentality.

It all starts from day one. Are you a cop or a professional police officer? I ask this all the time when I speak to both new and seasoned officers. And as I have said many times, I am not well liked in my own community of LEO, and at times I don't care.

Side note...I rattle the cage of what the standard of professional police officer must be. I remind my brothers and sisters who they swore they would be. And the thing I find the most ironic is that they don't need reminding, but they do...if that makes sense. They are the ones who have shown me the example, as I have said, and I am simply holding the mirror back up to their faces and showing them who they are. I am beyond passionate about being a professional police officer and have no issue making enemies to weed out who can't rise to the task.

The problem house with the gentleman who we've arrested countless times for fighting with his wife and then us, will most likely take one look at you, if you are brand new, and tear you apart the first time he meets you. He just knows that you are new and can smell it on you. This just has everything to do with your command presence or lack of.

Does that mean you step up and "show him who's boss"? Absolutely not.

It means you use what you are good at, learn from the call, and develop yourself into the officer you want to become. I am a firm believer in keeping your mouth shut on calls and letting those who are handling it, handle it.

The concept of "contact and cover officers" is just that. A contact officer makes contact and runs the call, while a cover officer shuts his/her mouth and provides alert cover. But I digress.

So many times in my career, I have been disappointed in those who were supposedly there to lead me, as well as been upset with myself for not stepping up to the plate and leading. It's a two-way street and a dynamic responsibility of balance.

Just because someone is wearing bars on their collar or cloverleafs does not mean they are qualified to lead others. By now, I am sure we are all familiar with the first episode of Band of Brothers.

I know I am randomly spouting off thoughts on this topic, but it is a dynamic topic, to begin with. The concept is just very important to me, and I hold it to the highest standards of being a good police officer.

THE PUBLIC

Going back to this category in leadership, you must make sure your interaction with the public is at the very paramount of integrity for all that you do. Not only will they see and respond to you and your actions, but so will your co-workers. If you are not the standard of integrity, it will be seen, and it will be noted by all.

From traffic stops to domestics to consensual encounters, you must ask yourself and answer honestly, "Am I the standard of a police officer that I would want to interact with my closest loved ones?"

Doesn't matter if that speeder just flew past you and you

were just putting a sandwich in your mouth. You have no right to storm up to the car and yell.

Doesn't matter if you were just about to end your tour and a ridiculous domestic comes over the air, and you've been to the house twice already in the last week, you have no right to walk in and just start barking at them.

And I couldn't care less if you just saw a dead child on your last call and you stopped a woman who didn't have her toddler secured in his safety seat the right way, you have no right to take your emotions out on her.

Is this easy? Not a chance in hell. Do I violate my own standards? All the time.

But then again, I am not in my 20's anymore, and as a man in my 40's, I have seen enough and felt enough to finally understand that a person's perception is their reality.

We are the lucky ones.

We are the ones who were chosen, among thousands, to do a job that demands our utmost personal best. People literally depend on us for solutions to problems that they just cannot handle on their own. Do you, as a new or even seasoned officer, take the time to reflect on that?

I have a huge level of pride that supports an even larger ego. It is almost impossible for me to call for help with a problem I may have. I think about that when I think about people who truly look to us in their times of need.

They swallow their pride, they pick up that phone, and they call 911. And if it is not an emergency, almost nine out of ten times they say, "I am really sorry and don't mean to waste your time."

Last time I checked, they are our time, and nothing is a waste of it.

The police and the public have a relationship. They HAVE to have one.

I strongly suggest you read, Sir Robert Peel's Nine Principles of Policing and return to the source material of where our ideals and standards began.

Look, the public may hate us from time to time, with this being one of the worst times in our history for their hate, but if one thing in relationships holds true, it's that communication is the life source of its success.

We must communicate with our public, and there are many ways to do so. Don't forget, there is verbal and non-verbal communication.

Non-verbal communication is your command presence, your body language, the look on your face, etc. It's all the little things that you may not think about.

To all new guys, I try to make it known that I am not a fan of an officer driving around in his/her squad car with the window open and their arm resting on it. TO ME, that gives off a carefree look to the public and not one that says, "I am alert and earning the salary you are paying." To me, it just sends non-verbal communication of looking bad.

What about your uniform? Is it tailored, or is it too big for you? Is your shirt bloused or do you use "shirt stays?" Boots polished? Are you fit, or are you fat? No, I will not sugar coat my dialogue to coddle your feelings. If you are fat, you are fat, trust me, there was a time where I was too, and neither myself, my partners, nor my town deserved to see me out of shape.

I am very public about my views on police and fitness.

To my knowledge, outside of the standard physical testing that we have to pass to get hired (which is complete crap), there is no requirement that has us keeping a level of fitness throughout our career.

I recall a Chief of Police in some southern state, several years ago, who was ousted by his guys after a vote of no confidence due to him trying to implement a fitness policy that resulted in discipline.

Sorry folks, but don't you want fit police officers showing up at your door to help you? Or do you want to be left standing and facing the bad guy after the officer dropped dead of a heart attack while attempting to take the offender into custody?

Bottom line, fitness is a professional standard in our profession that should and must be addressed. Actually, it's a damn shame that it even has to be addressed in the first place. But, it is what it is in a world of unions and crybabies I guess.

My passion is connecting the police with the public by any means.

You'll hear me refer to Sir Robert Peel's 9 Principles of Policing often, with one being, "The police are the public and the public are the police."

This, to me, is a shared responsibility for both entities to maintain the integrity and responsibility of the community and the love we have for one another. Idealistic? You bet, but then again, that's what I am, an idealist.

The issue today is that the police are not seen as holding up our end of that agreement. SEEN…and that "seen" has been generated by the media and others who have their own agenda, resulting in such distinct segregation of both of us, the public and the police.

I could go on all day about the Generation X and Y members who failed to raise men and women and how we are a society of victims. But this book is about the police and the responsibility from our end. In my view, we are the strong ones who can handle the burden, and we'll take it. After all, we signed up for this, right? I believe we did and we will not only weather the storm, but we will also navigate it for all.

Look, if I am redundant in what I am writing about, it's only because these are key points to the ideals that I feel are necessary for the integrity of policing.

When you think about it, we will come into contact with less than 3% of the population of any town on a daily basis. And that small percentage that we will come in contact with will be so due to a need that we must meet.

Again, and I have spoken about this before, their needs may not make sense to us, but they are their needs.

There are times when I take a step back and think to myself, "look… you have a job. You make good money and have a title of respect. Doesn't mean you are respected, but you have an opportunity to be respected every day. So many people that you will come in contact with neither have a job or the self-respect that goes with it as they are at such a point in their life of where they need 'something' that they called you for your service. It is my job to do my best to accept, respect, and act on the gift I have been given and truly practice my most powerful means of policing…I must care."

Yes, the idealist in me is my passion. I am a very emotional man who empathizes as best he can with everyone who counts on him.

It is beyond emotionally draining, and at times, I literally feel as if I can't move on my time off. I hurt. But that's a price I must pay for my own needs to be the man I want to be and the officer I know I swore to be.

Leadership is a very simple concept that I don't feel I really need to go into great depth over. Just do the right thing, all the time. Be the man/woman you would want to follow, and you will lead the right way.

It's been a very stormy 2015 through 2016 to this point, and if we are to proceed, improve, thrive, survive as a people, TOGETHER, I believe that we as police need to step up and be the leaders we are called to be.

ASK YOURSELF WHY

I've told a hand full of stories for the sake of you starting to get a feel for the dynamic of the job, but the point of this book is to cover the realities of it, in relation to both what the academy doesn't teach and or what you, the non-police person, kind of expect that we do. As well as hopefully give a new perspective to other officers for complimenting patrol tactics.

Most people who have no desire to do police work, still have an opinion on police officers and the expectations they are to have while serving their community. These expectations come from watching movies, cop shows, hearing first-person stories from police, hearing third-person stories from those who've interacted with the police or their own experience with the police. Oh, and social media, of course.

Bottom line is that everyone has formed an opinion of what the police should do.

My question to you, the non-police, is "Why?"

Why do you have an opinion as to what we should do? Granted, you are supposed to, and everyone has an opinion on every profession out there, but why have you formed yours, specifically about the police?

I know that I am asking a very loaded rhetorical question, but I do so in the hopes that you will start to see the job as a dynamic profession that requires your support as a non-police person. Ask "why" all you can and want. But please also ask yourself how you feel once you get the multi-faceted answer; especially the truth. Are you willing to accept the truth when you hear it or will your emotions blind you? We seem to be in an age where emotions are more important than facts. Don't let that be the case.

I pause here to make this point in the hopes that you will start to see that you, as a citizen, play a huge role in the lives of the officers who serve you. It's just as important for you to know who you are to us, as it is for you to know why we do what we do for you. I truly hope that makes sense and you embrace your role, as we are all in this together.

SOCIAL MEDIA AND THE POLICE

"I wonder how much more stoicism, impartiality, silence and 'police professionalism' our departments want us to display as yet more police officers are shot at, today.

Last time I checked, we are a family. And if your family is

attacked, you're allowed to show emotion.

Make no mistake, we are under attack, and I can't see how being "professional" is making this any better. More so, I can't see how going unheard is professional either.

I wish more people understood that there is no separating the private life of a police officer from their professional life. The pride we have for our profession and the people we serve are the seamless adhesive that makes us who we are versus the cowardice and evil of those who are attacking us.

I, for one, won't ever separate the two and you bet damn well that my life and my family's lives in blue, matter more than theirs. Now, command staff, they separate the two for policy needs. That's called control.

When I write on social media, it is meant to express my opinion as a man, who happens to have tremendous pride in serving my town and country.

But even as an individual, my heart breaks for being expected to just stay vigilant and "rise above" all of this.

Praying that a leader steps up and calls us Warriors to action soon. – Facebook post from the Officer Dominick Izzo page, March 14th, 2016."

I had written this post after reading that three Chicago police officers had been shot at, with two being wounded, in a post on my Facebook feed. The day before, a Maryland officer was shot and killed at his police department in an ambush by three brothers, again, as seen on my Facebook feed.

Several days prior to this incident, I had received an update to our department's policy, regarding social media posting and the prohibiting of wearing police attire that could identify any of us as members of the police department. This policy was directly put in place due to me and the "Officer Dominick Izzo" page on Facebook and the attention it was getting.

According to command, a representative of the Black Lives Matter movement had called my village with a nonspecific complaint that I was a racist. And in a meeting with command, they had stated that they could never verify the person's credibility with being associated with BLM or even what the complaint was.

My command had scoured my Facebook and not seen a single indication of any race-related posting on my end. They had concluded that the claim was invalid and unsubstantiated. Yet, a few days later, new additions to the policy on social media were added. The additions stated that no longer are personnel allowed to post videos or pictures of themselves in attire that either was the department's official uniform or attire that could be mistaken as such.

Furthermore, any opinionated posts on social media forums must have a disclaimer of them being the opinion of the person as an individual and not as a representative of the department or town they worked for.

I had had a lengthy discussion with my commanders that day, which I argued that separation of an officer's private life and professional life just isn't possible in today's world of social media and the damage it will cause is looming around the corner.

The departments look at policy regulation as liability and litigation prevention, and I look at it as a general order telling me to disassociate myself with my department in my personal life… "We don't want to be associated with you" is how I emotionally took it, and it just re-enforces the pain when members of our family get attacked. Especially in times when we all need to come together and show pride for what we do.

The point, or at least the general usage of social media, is to show the best of yourself. No one goes online and posts about how miserable their life is, granted we post about problems and whatnot, but we all try to create our images of our very best in character.

That said, I for one want to show my passion and pride in service for the town I care for. For service to them is MY personal best. It's who I am the proudest of being.

For me, there is no separation of my private life and the profession I chose. I can understand how departments may want their officers to not show sides of them that have them boozing it up in the bars and then write DUI's all night long or the officers who talk nothing about MMA fights and then suspiciously rack up resisting arrest charges against every offender they come in contact with.

I get the negative association with Facebook and the officers who aren't mature enough to comprehend their responsibilities, but that is what supervision, documentation, discipline and termination are for…and I support it all.

No, the academy didn't warn me about nature of politics in policing and how they mix with my emotions, nor the times when I would have to pick and choose my battles over what was right in my heart versus what the brass stated was gospel. And that is a lesson I still am horrible at learning.

Understand something, social media WILL help destroy the police.

But not as we know and use it now. It's the lack of us using social media that will cause our demise as a nation of proud police who serve our people.

Fear is what drives both the public perception of the police and the agencies who write policies against the police using social media.

All it takes is a clip of the week in a Facebook feed and some officer's 30 second interaction of a five minute encounter with a subject and that officer becomes the new lamb led to the slaughter while the subject in question runs to the nearest lawyer's office to strategize his next paycheck…and village admins are circling the wagons as fast as they can to prevent this. I don't blame them at all, but there is an effective way to combat this. USE SOCIAL MEDIA.

The village fears a payout, the officer fears for his job and being abandoned by the village and the world fears we have nothing but bad cops out there.

Why? Because that's all we are allowed to see on social media.

Social media restriction was/is designed to prevent the characterization and imagery of those who post themselves in bars getting drunk, those who make irresponsible statements without thinking, those who repost inappropriate humor or hate, all which do not represent the standards for which they were hired under. Again, I understand this.

Social media restriction guidelines are meant to hold officers to the highest standards possible while representing the agencies they work for in their personal time.

But do they?

Defense attorneys are chomping at the bit to use social media for their needs.

"Your honor...as you can see, Officer Izzo is not a Green Bay Packer fan. He posted a comment last night about the Packer's being a losing team that he hates. And my client has a Packer bumper sticker on his car. THAT is the reason Officer Izzo stopped my client, wrote him a DUI and injured my client as he took him into custody and not because my client's blood-alcohol level was a .274 and that he physically attacked Officer Izzo, causing the officer to respond in kind."

These will be the new character attacks against the police used to dismiss criminals from the responsibility of their actions and behavior.

Why? Because the police will not be able to use social media to their advantage and show the good in what we do in both our personal lives that co-exist with our professional lives. Why would anyone want to see that Officer Smith is a huge advocate of juvenile interaction and he is seen in countless pictures and videos of himself playing, talking, counseling, mentoring and just being around the kids of his town, in uniform and on duty, ON HIS SOCIAL MEDIA PAGE?

Defense attorneys wouldn't. They wouldn't want to challenges any case that comes into play where Officer Smith was seen in the most positive aspects of dealing with juveniles if, as an example, a juvenile offender accused Officer Smith of malice and ill intent towards him. Because the overwhelming proof of character would show otherwise and the defense would have to do their job just like the police and prosecution do and go off of FACTS instead of assumptions for a change.

When a criminal goes before a judge (let's use bond hearings as an example) the judge, often times wants to hear the status of the criminal's financial ability to determine if bond will be cash or personal recognizance. Imagine a drug dealer caught with heroin.

If the judge hears that the subject deals drugs and got caught and that's all the information the judge knows, a cash bond will be set.

But...

If the judge learns that the subject deals drugs because he has a newborn, he lost his job, is three months behind on rent, his wife has cancer, and he is desperate, he will most likely be released on his own signature.

Can you see the difference in character?

This happens all the time.

Turn on the news and see some gang member who killed someone in a shooting... what picture does the media use? A high-school cap and gown photo instead of the one where he is on his Facebook throwing up gang signs and holding a gun.

This double-edged sword intensifies and sharpens for the police.

An officer is already damned, no matter what he/she posts because lawyers are looking at every single angle to discredit us.

If we humanize ourselves and post about our breakup, family problems, health concerns, financial status, etc., the lawyer will say that our actions against their clients have a bias or the officer wasn't fit to do his/her job. And if the village saw this post and let the officer work their tour that day, they are liable too.

HOWEVER...

Lack of social media presence, lack of social media associated with our profession (no posting in uniform, no police expressive narratives, etc.) leads to a total and complete separation of work and personal life...and no longer the officer viewing his/her job as a profession or lifestyle, but rather a means to a paycheck within the hours of service and the limits of their personal agenda. Do you as a resident want that?

If the world isn't allowed to see us in our uniform, representing the honor, integrity, and pride of what we worked so hard to be a part of, then where will the officer's humanity end and the Police Officer robot begin?

Without the humanization of the officer, the argument can be made that we are infallible.

And if we are infallible, then every decision made under time and pressure MUST be the right one.

Every round shot must hit the target with surgical precision.

Every arrest must be righteous, every citizen contact without error, and every tour ended without the loss of life or injury.

Yes, all of those things are what we currently strive for. But it's while we are still humans who act and train with the passion of our chosen profession.

Lack of social media associated with a person and their passion for their profession creates robots who can never be human and can never err. Causing not the highest level of standard, but a model of drone-like expectations that will be used in future liberal arguments to prove that policing as a whole needs to be completely re-evaluated.

And that's where our standard will be set, failed to be met and destroyed.

Furthermore, what is the risk of officers not doing their job?

When will the mentality of "I'm not on the clock" begin when an off duty cop drives past an accident for fear of misrepresenting their department against policy because he had a tee-shirt on that said "POLICE" and someone was filming him/her helping at the scene or getting sued because they acted and the motorist wants a quick dollar?

Why aren't agencies using the power of social media as their bridge with their residents?

Why aren't their officer bios on every department Facebook page?

Safety? Sure...if an officer doesn't want their information out there, that's fine.

But what about transparency and pride?

What about an officer bio on Facebook that shows the officer's passion for the department, the town, the people...

Take it a step further and offer full transparency and show complaints, commendations, complaint resolutions, education and training, disciplinary actions, etc. all about the officer so that the people of the town not only know what their taxes pay for but give them full association with who they hired and trust to protect them, creating a sense of COMMUNITY.

Not for nothing, but if I'm shot and bleeding in a ditch line, I want someone recognizing me as Officer Izzo from Facebook and running to use my radio to call for help.

Policy changes are coming.

They will remove the pride of being a police officer and focus on the blurred line of where the passion ends, and the job begins...and that's going to be when the officer isn't on the clock.

Without the connection of a man or woman and the passion they have for policing your town, you will have an employee who shows up to work, does the minimum and clocks out.

Pride in this job is almost as important as the oath we swore. And you want/need your officers proud of who they are, for it brings out their best.

As of now, the liberal media is the only one creating the image of the police, as departments and policy are limiting the necessary fighting back we need to do to show the truth.

If you're passionate about your profession or the officers who serve your town, then meet with your department command staff and create a policy that allows the pride to be shown through.

Right now, the driving force behind policy is liability and litigation.

Let's try and change that to character, integrity, and a proud standard of shown excellence.

We must be active on social media, showing the positive, engaging, and educational side of what we do as police officers and ambassadors of our communities.

We must post with pride and integrity, exercising our best character within our first amendment right and showing our department(s) the positive and productive influence social media has for us.

Throw me up on the stand any day of the week and question my character...social media has allowed me a tremendous platform to show how much I love the town, department and people I work for.

Other officers and admins need to embrace this platform themselves.

Chapter Seventeen

EVER CHANGING TIMES AND YOUR PLACE IN IT

THE CHANGE

There is so much to write, so much the public needs to know on how we were affected and how they are impacted from inept and unethical men/women who they allow to be placed into leadership.

The goal, mission, and purpose of this book and subsequent books are for one reason…the public and the police must work together and find accountability in one another.

Change is coming, one way or another. But I believe with all my heart that the American Police Officer will be the one title that holds true in the strength of integrity and pioneers that change with a righteous effect on all they serve.

And in the spring of 2017, having lost all faith in those who are promised change-makers, I announced that I was running for Sheriff of the Cook County Sheriff's Department in Illinois.

The David vs. Goliath fight began.

I am still in a pending lawsuit with my former department, and the outcome is in the hands of the court and God, with my faith in both of them.

On July 29th, at our nation's capital, with my backdrop being the Capitol Building itself, I stood on a platform, with mic in hand, addressed a crowd of our Nation's greatest patriots, and promised them with my winning the office of Sheriff, I would change the world… so get ready.

And welcome to the change.

2019 AND THE END

No, I didn't win the election. Hell, I didn't even make it on the ballot. But I fought until the very end like I swore I would. I am toying with the idea of running again in 2022, but who knows.

I entered law enforcement in March of 2001, not expecting what it would do to me or if I would have any impact on it. Hell, back then I was too respectful to think that any single one of us could have an impact on the entirety of law enforcement on it's whole; nearly 19 years later and it's even with a greater respect that I tell you that you MUST impact law enforcement if you are to have called yourself a cop to begin with.

And it was in October of 2019 where I put the badge down for the last and final time.

After a near 3 year legal war, the status of "termination" was removed from name and I was fully reinstated as a police officers and officially retired with a clear and good standing. The fight was long and hard, but it was necessary and I am continuing to fight on a new, different and more powerful front.

I began my law enforcement career in March of 2001 and ended it in October of 2019. I have absolutely no regrets with any of it. Not the relationships I made, those I lost, the battles I fought on the streets and within the department(s). I look back on my years of service with reflection of great pride and integrity. I was a great cop.

I now fight forward with a greater sense of pride, integrity and willingness to serve with all that I have gained along the way by helping those who still wear the badge, wore the badge or heed their calling to wear it.

Many ask if the fight against it all was worth it and I tell them this; with all that I am, I would do it all again. When we fight for our integrity, we are fighting to secure our legacy. And I continue to build mine.

Being a cop was the greatest job I ever had. You will see that if and when the time comes, you truly will. And if it doesn't you will understand why YOU are the job and you have the capability to make your ultimate calling the greatest job you'll ever have as well. It's contradictory, I know. But in the end you define the badge or title, it doesn't define you.

But, should you wear the badge, know this:

You will change, grow, love, hurt, hate, break and heal... and you will be more alive than you can imagine.

In the end, the badge number you wear on your chest will go to someone else. You will either resign, retire or get fired and you will be "you" again, a person without a number pinned to your chest and for many that loss is impossible to handle or understand. But the rub of it is, that you always were you, that badge never was you. But again, in time, you will get what I am saying.

Do not lose hope your in humanity. Yes, people are beyond evil, yes, they are lost and you will be exposed to being at the risk of losing yourself while serving them.

But hold fast and be vigilant. Be the light, the shield and when needs be, the sword.

Swear an oath the United States Constitution, your state and your city, but more so, swear it to yourself.

Be you, always. And know this...

Love will never win, nor will it get the job done. That is just a fact that you will have to get used to. You will see what I mean as the years pass. The support will come and disappear, just as fast as you think it will. You will learn how the "brotherhood" doesn't exist. But that doesn't mean you cannot be the example that others aspire to as a singular holder of the Thin Blue Line.

Throughout your journey you will be respected and valued, and betrayed and left alone to fight alone both by the public and your brothers and sisters in blue. This is just the nature of the job and has existed since the dawn of man's wicked and selfish ways.

But, remember that you are not the job, you are you and you are upholding the integrity of millions who came before you and you are setting the standard for millions who will come after you, so make your mark. I speak very cynically now, but at the root of my words still flow the idealism of the love and honor that you must promise yourself to never lose.

Yes, all of that which is negative will come your way. But if you are ready for it, you will not break. You will remain fortified and a stronghold of hope.

Love doesn't get the job done, but in the end love is all you have, because it is what you were made from.

Without the infinity of that concept and the blessing of the promise of each and every new day, there is no life… and life is what you are here to serve and protect.

I love you all like family and will forever be indebted to you for all that you do. For whether or not you even know it, you have done more for me than you can ever know. And someday I may get the honor of shaking your hand and let you know how.

In our King, Jesus Christ's name; be safe always, go home to your family every night, keep everyone safe if you can no matter who they are or what they've done.

Never lie no matter the cost, even if it costs you your job.

Believe in the truth of the job and in the depths of your Soul that you will always do the right thing.

Fight and never ever give up, live with ruthless passion and righteous truth.

Love others and yourself with intensity, ferocity and unrestraint.

And above all, be thankful and humble that God called you to be a Police Officer and you answered Him, or know that when the time comes and He does call, you will answer with ardent conviction.

Know you are valued, loved, respected and honored by me and many. And know that you are never, ever alone. Now make us all proud.

Be safe, Officer.
Izzo

APPENDIX I

The following are both the letters I sent him and to the mayor, with no response given, other than my termination.

DEMAND LETTER OF RESIGNATION

Chief George Filenko,

The following is a request by the officers of the Round Lake Park Police Department for your formal resignation as Chief of Police for the Village of Round Lake Park.

This request is submitted due to your inability to properly command the Round Lake Park Police Department, your contribution to the inner conflict among officers, the promoting of hostile work environment, including divisiveness, threats, rumors, spreading of gossip, unbecoming conduct as well as your personal policy violations and derelict of duty, display of nepotism and preferential treatment, including but not limited to the allowing of potential criminal conduct of officers as well as intentional neglect of required discipline to correct conduct of officers.

After numerous memos and meetings with you, it is on behalf of the officers, expressing a concern for more structured leadership from the office of Chief of Police. It is with the current relationship between the police and public we serve, including the frequent excelled loss of life among police officers throughout the nation, we, the officers of the Village of Round Lake Park, have no confidence in your ability to lead properly, ethically, morally or conduct yourself in the professional manner required to match the standard set by the citizens of the Village of Round Lake Park.

Furthermore, the incidents involving your command staff's inability to properly and professionally lead the officers of the

Round Lake Park Police Department (including intimidation, inability to address illegal / immoral officer activity and the failure to recognize unbecoming conduct from officers), is a direct reflection of your inability to command efficiently, failing also to meet the needs of the officers' requirements to best serve the citizens of the Village of Round Lake Park.

Sir, please be advised of the following reasons:

- Hostile work environment including swearing/threatening at personnel
    - Observed daily ongoing use of foul language to and at officers, ostracizing officers, derogatory and inflammatory language, rumor and gossip spreading
- Offensive physical body contact
    - Documented incidents of threatening, unwanted, offensive, and insulting physical contact
- Openly discussing sexual activity between employees
    - Documented incidents of personal inappropriate and offensive sexual remarks, including failure to address regarding the same conduct
- Discrimination (religious) (nationality) (age)
    - Observed and documented vocal prejudice against officer's religious choice, heritage and age, including racial and insulting comments
- Consistent involvement in ongoing lawsuit/litigation
    - E. Tjarksen / Bonaroti / Officers of the Village of Round Lake Park
- Priority focus on state/county police activity, including personal agenda
    - Observed priority focus on Lake County police activ-

Appendix I

ity, habitual absence from Round Lake Park, priority on personal business, i.e., lectures, book publication, interviews

Proven history of inability to maintain self-control (anger management)

2008 Order to attend anger management / observed continued inability to control anger and hostility via physical and very actions, i.e., door slamming, name-calling, swearing to and at officers, vulgarity and slander

Inability to maintain the integrity of legal investigative evidence

Department body camera evidence released to internet websites

Lacking in legitimate police experience

No known credible/legitimate patrol or community policing history

Drawing consistent negative national attention to the police department

Negative focus of FBI investigations, lawsuits, scrutiny over Gliniewicz / Calusinski investigations / current Watchguard body camera investigation

Inability to maintain structure of command staff including the allowing of intimidation

Allowance of personal and intimate relationship between commanding officer and subordinate officer, allowance of threats and intimidation by commanding officer to subordinate officers, after written notification to your office

Based on the aforementioned, it is our demand that you be

immediately replaced by an interim Police Chief to restore the public trust, the department trust, restore the Police Officers' perceived safety, the Police Department's integrity and protect the reputation set forth by the standards outlined in the Round Lake Park Police Department Mission Statement.

We request the Village of Round Lake Park board work with the officers to ensure a structured growth, integrity and increased level of accountability from the Round Lake Park Police Department in order to meet and exceed the needs of the Village of Round Lake Park as a whole.

Respectfully,
Ofc Dominick Izzo #501

Appendix I

LETTER TO MAYOR LINDA LUCASSEN

Letter 1:

11/22/2016

Mayor Lucassen,

Ms. Mayor, I am submitting to you, via attachment, the demand letter of resignation issued to Chief George Filenko on November 21st, 2016 from myself on behalf of numerous officers in the Round Lake Park Police Department.

It is my most sincere wish that the content of the resignation letter to Mr. Filenko as well as the content of this letter to yourself, be received as imploringly heartfelt with the most honorable intentions accompanying it.

Ms. Mayor, on December 3rd of this year, I will have completed my 3rd year of proud service for the Village of Round Lake Park.

I was honored to come to you after serving for two other villages over several years and bringing my passion to public service to our village, which I have so proudly called home.

I have proudly respected my nature as a champion for just righteousness and as an enemy of police corruption, proving my word through actions by standing up to my previous police departments' conduct of unethical and immoral activity.

I believe that my strong history of public service, duty performance, highly visible international advocating of community relationships as well as personal integrity towards truth and acting as a standard model for the Village of Round Lake Park as a Police Officer, has been not only evident but acknowledged and respected by the Mayor's office.

My passion and love for police and community lives deep within the Village of Round Lake Park and springs forward throughout the nation in attempts to learn, grow and become more in order to return to our citizens, standing proud and tall as a guardian, confidant, enforcer, advocate, aid, mentor, pillar, wall and mirror to those who live with us and see in me the reflection of who they could call Officer.

It is and always has been my first and most focused mission, as a police officer for the Village of Round Lake Park, to uphold the most intimate and expectant needs of our citizens…to live with un-obscured freedom.

Freedom from the evil of man through immoral, unethical, and criminal action; both from the outside public and within the very government of whom they entrust to protect them.

Ms Mayor, it is with the greatest and most humble respect that I am compelled to come to you as a witness from within the walls of the Round Lake Park Police department as I have personally observed and been given attested, credible, damaging and damning information of the abusive, neglectful, immoral, unethical and criminal activity which has been the direct contribution of Chief George Filenko.

It is the unacceptable behavior from Mr. Filenko, whose primary and highly visible focus on all activity outside of the village, has left an inner collapse of structure, resulting in the unethical and immoral behavior such as officers engaging in illegal arrests, officers violating citizen's civil rights, officers failing to receive proper and incomplete training, officers serving against the recommendation via command and trainer personnel, officers with scarce police experience supervising each other on high-risk shifts with no senior or command guidance.

Furthermore, it is the direct derelict of duty from Mr. Filenko that as attributed to threatening, illegal and unethical conduct of command personnel, including inappropriate and sexual relationships between officers, nepotism, favoritism and discrimination.

Mr. Filenko's primary focus over his tenure as police chief has been involved in Lake County activity outside of the Village of Round Lake Park's needs, as clearly can be observed in his absence, his prioritizing and his lack of ability to run the operations of the police department.

The Village of Round Lake Park requires an involved and

intimate police force, setting the standard of service, which includes not only the enforcement of law but the respect and compassion to the quality of life of which those in our care deserve.

Ms. Mayor, the heavy-handed and most dispassionate display set forth by your police officers is not only unacceptable, yet dangerous in this time of public mistrust.

Our Police force must be the humble and strong example of safety and service that our people expect, and currently, under the failed command of George Filenko, the residents of Round Lake Park are subject to punishment, fines, harassment and fear, all with their voices being gone unheard and disrespected.

As you know, I am subject to discipline, including termination for my involvement in disseminating department property without the permission of the office of the Chief of Police. And while I am able to justify, qualify and answer to the nature of my actions, I still act as a servant for the Village of Round Lake Park until I am dismissed and this includes the continuing in the oath I swore to serve our citizens by combating illegal, unjust, immoral and unethical behavior.

To date, nearly twenty (20) police officers have left the Village of Round Lake Park while under the command of George Filenko without being given exit interviews to the board. Testimony of bullying, harassment, hospitalization, threats, and ostracizing have all been at the core of each issue.

Numerous lawsuits have had George Filenko as the center of focus while he has been entrusted as a public servant.

National negative attention of criminal investigations have had George Filenko as the focus, drawing the unwanted attention to the Village of Round Lake Park.

The Round Lake Park Police Department is one of the few agencies, nationwide, which is allowed to run at an almost "free for all" capacity, with officers being held to subjective standards to fit the needs of George Filenko's disciplinary discretion and failed structure.

This is due to the direct attribution of George Filenko having had no prior credible or valid police experience. Being appointed to the office of Chief of Police by the mayor's office after serving as a dispatcher has proven to be damaging beyond Mr. Filenko's ability to reconcile or control.

Unqualified and uneducated officers have been allowed to rule over our citizens, and commanders appointed to supervise without proper training or knowledge.

Illegal, immoral and unethical activity has all been allowed to cultivate and thrive within the bounds of the Village of Round Lake Park, all due to the attribution of the Office of Chief of Police, under the command of George Filenko, held unaccountable by the Mayor's office and lack of public scrutiny.

Ms. Mayor, it is my immediate request that you support and demand my continued service within the Village of Round Lake Park as a police officer, including considering my role in a leadership capacity as I am convicted that my standards of excellence, ability and guided morals will bring prosperity and growth to both the police department and to the residents of the Village or Round Lake Park.

Furthermore, it is my request that you immediately remove and replace George Filenko as Chief of Police and replace the office with a person of integrity, knowledge, honor, public respect, public trust and a proven history in his ability to lead.

Hindered, persecuted and oppressed within the village due to his highly visible public adoration, ability and proven credible history as a law enforcement officer, I strongly urge you to look past the one-sided and slanderous reputation that George Filenko has portrayed of Officer Joe Segreti.

It has been in several, personal and private conversations with George Filenko, during a time where I was both his confidant and his pupil, where Joe Segreti was highly praised by Filenko as both the standard model of a public servant and as a "brilliant" police officer.

However, it was in those same conversations where Mr. Filenko voiced to me his lengthy disdain for Officer Segreti and

Appendix I

his personal intent to oppress Segreti's career while under Filenko's command due to a difference in their personal history.

It is in my most professional and experienced opinion, as well as a developed respect for Officer Joe Segreti that his ability to lead our department towards a promised future is only surpassed by his passion and adoration for the people within the village. And I respectfully request that all the Mayor must do to validate my statement is to walk the town and ask the people themselves.

It is my greatest desire to continue to help and heal the Round Lake Park Police Department and our citizens during this tumultuous time in our nation's history. I believe with all of my heart that we can be the center of the standard of excellence that America and the world see as to how Police Officers are to truly serve.

Respectfully,
Ofc Dominick Izzo #501

Letter 2:

Mayor Lucassen,

It has been brought to my attention that a letter of confidence in Chief George Filenko was drafted by Officer Donna O'Brien and signed by every officer except for Officer Joe Segreti and myself.

I submit to you the following information, moving forward, for yourself and the village board to use at your discretion.

As I have stated in written documents, there have been illegal activities, unethical and immoral behavior, bullying, and threatening behavior within your department. I submit to you the following and leave it to you to act on or leave as is, however, hope your oath of office as mayor compels you to take action.

Hostile work environment, including threatening behavior:

> It has been an almost daily observation by myself, and Officer Lyons (who confides in myself and other officers that he is afraid to speak out for fear of retaliation from George Filenko) of Chief Filenko's daily foul and insulting language. His orders of "get the fuck in your office" "why the fuck are you not on the road," and other use of expletive language have been tolerated only due to the fact that there is no course of action for the chief violating his own department General Order (here forth referenced as GO) CONDUCT 3-1 IV Unbecoming Conduct A. 4. Offensive Language. This common use of language by Chief Filenko has caused myself and other officers to be uncomfortable due not to the language, however Chief Filenko's familiarity and ease with said usage to those he commands over. This, in my opinion, is unprofessional and has root towards his other issues.
>
> I submit the following instances as proof of threatening behavior by both Chief George Filenko and Commander Hec-

Appendix I

tor Lepe and request the board further look into the matter:

1) Immediate state charge issuance and suspension of Commander Tony Colon on 06/25/16 after the filing of the federal lawsuit on 06/23/16.

To the department personnel's knowledge, Commander Tony Colon served nearly 10 years with the Round Lake Park Police Department, had no known prior disciplinary action, was a former member of Lake County MEG, the department FTO, K9 officer, detective and supervisory commander.

Commander Colon was in possession of his department-issued cell phone for approximately 6 years (as was Commander Lepe) and had received no prior orders or discipline for misuse. I submit to the mayor that she and the board acknowledge the direct correlation of Chief Filenko's blatant retaliation to Commander Colon for his involvement in the federal lawsuit. I furthermore submit that during a meeting with our attorney, we were advised that the disciplinary hearing attorney for the Village of Round Lake Park advised Commander Colon's attorney, that Chief Filenko stated, "I want him (Colon) gone."

I submit this action on Chief Filenko's part was intentional, malicious, and for the purpose of intimidation and threatening behavior to all other officers in the lawsuit. I ask the village board why an upstanding, award receiving officer, commander and leader was issued such discipline in such a closely related time to the discovery of nefarious activity linked to Chief Filenko.

2) I was advised by both John Shepard and Walter Rodrigues that they both removed themselves from the lawsuit due to testing for St Charles Police Department and Mundelein Police Department after having a private meeting with

Chief Filenko and did not want to hinder their lateral hires due to their involvement.

3) I was advised by Christopher Valle that he removed his name from the lawsuit after a private meeting with Chief Filenko due to his fear as a probationary officer for losing his job. Furthermore, Valle was immediately removed from his FTO by myself and placed with Deputy Chief Burch as an action of unprofessionalism and retaliation towards myself as a field training officer.

4) On May 14th, 2016, after notifying yourself (Mayor Lucassen, at your residence) of the body camera discovery, I began getting phone calls from numerous Round Lake Park Police Officers who all advised me of the same statement, "chief is calling me. He said you've fucking lost it and he's going to have the FBI investigate you." I believe this to be fact as you, yourself were attached in a department email which was CC'd to Commanders Lepe and Colon, which stated Chief Filenko's intent to have me investigated by the FBI which was also advised to me by Lepe and Colon. This threatening action by Chief Filenko caused me great stress, as my Chief, instead of investigating the accusations, directly accused me of involvement, including to proceed to lock me out of my department email for a period of four (4) days.

During a private conversation with Chief Filenko, during June of 2016, after removing all body cameras and server, while in the parking lot of 215 E Main St, Chief Filenko leaned his body in my squad car and stated, "We're good, right?" He extended his hand to shake and then stated to me, as he tightly gripped my hand, "I've been through worse, and I always win" as he smiled at me and entered into the building. Chief Filenko had one further private conversation with me at 215 E Main St, in the conference room, which can be verified by Officer Lyons in that Chief Filenko praised me as both an officer and as a man.

Appendix I

I submit this as either tactical manipulative behavior or mental health issues which must be addressed with Chief Filenko.

5) Commander Hector Lepe requested his removal from the federal lawsuit after he had been the recipient of threatening behavior and intimidation by Chief George Filenko on an ongoing basis, which can be verified by Tony Colon, Matthew Lyons, Joe Segreti and myself, as Lepe confided in all of us with the same information in summary.

Lepe was brought up on state charges on or about 08/04/16 for using his department cellphone to view pornography while on duty.

Lepe made the statement that he accepted all accusations against himself while in his interrogation and was notified he would receive his discipline within ten (10) days. To date, Lepe has received no discipline and has removed himself from the lawsuit after being intimated and pressured by Chief Filenko. I can and will provide text message proof of my personal and intimate relationship with Lepe as he confided in me via phone, text and personal conversations of his disapproval, dislike and sought after dismissal of Chief Filenko as well as that he was being pressured by Chief Filenko to drop the lawsuit and increase discipline on myself and other officers.

I ask the village to inquire why Commander Colon was disciplined whereas Commander Lepe was not unless Commander Lepe was/is a tool for Chief Filenko to administer disciplinary action and influence other officers to exit the federal lawsuit.

I can provide a timeline for the recent discipline that I, myself, received at the hand of Lepe after he advised me on 10/22/16, while in the parking lot of 215 E Main St, "It's in your best interest to drop out of the lawsuit" and "I don't know what they (Chief Filenko and Deputy Chief Burch) are going to do to you…I am going to do what I have to do to keep my job."

Shortly after I received three (3) counts of discipline, which I submitted for grievance to your office in step two and then the notice of interrogation the day after the submitted step two.

I submit that after my years of service to the Round Lake Park Police Department, my Chief, Filenko, issued awards, history of documented performance, community accolades and letters of commendation from outside agencies. I submit this as obvious and blatant retaliation as I have been the target in the progressive list for Chief Filenko to remove officers from the federal lawsuit via intimidation, retaliation and terminations. I have documented all of the following and submitted it to our attorney for his attention at retaliatory employer conduct and violation of the federal whistleblower act.

I believe the village board will take the time to systematically timeline the events I have documented and see this is an indisputable fact.

Offensive Physical Body Conduct

In the summer of 2015 and 2016 I was the recipient of unwanted and offensive physical body contact by Chief George Filenko in that on two (2) separate occasions, while at 215 E Main St in the rear portion of the police department, he placed his hand(s) on my stomach area, pushed in and asked me, "what the fuck is this? Are you getting fat?" Furthermore, I have observed Chief Filenko make this same statement to John Shepard and Matthew Lyons.

During the summer of 2016, while advising me of a police-involved shooting, Chief Filenko while at the rear portion of 215 E Main St, placed his left hand on my right shoulder and stated to me, "you know, it's just a matter of time before a cop gets shot here" as he shook my shoulder and smiled at me. I believe this to have been an indirect threatening statement towards myself or other officers for entering the federal lawsuit.

In doing the above, Chief Filenko has violated GO CONDUCT 3-1 IV. Unbecoming Conduct A. 10. Harassment (1) (b) and (c) based on the unwanted and offensive physical body contact and GO CONDUCT 3-1 IV Unbecoming Conduct 5 Political Influence, as I submit that Chief Filenko used his office of chief status to threaten me during the time of the filed federal lawsuit.

Openly Discussing Sexual Activity

In the conference room at 215 E Main St during 2014, I observed Chief Filenko make a statement to Deputy Chief Dan Burch wherein Chief Filenko, in the presence of myself, Burch, Tony Colon, and Hector Lepe stated, "you're fucking her (Donna O'Brien) aren't you!?"

This is a violation of GO 3-1 IV. 9. 1. Prohibited activity in its entirety for verbal sexual harassment.

Discrimination (Age) (Nationality) (Religious)

I have observed, on several occasions, while at 215 E Main St, Chief Filenko make comments to Hector Lepe, regarding his Hispanic heritage, in statements such as, "Do you even speak English? What the fuck?" "You write your fucking reports like you speak broken English."

I have been the recipient of Chief Filenko's statements

while in his office at 215 E Main St, "I agree with your writings (in regard to Facebook political posts) but I don't agree with your Jesus bullshit" and has commented while laughing, "what the fuck are those?" while pointing to my tattoos depicting Christ.

I have been the direct recipient of comments during conversations with both Chief Filenko and Deputy Chief Dan Burch, while at 215 E Main St, as well as unsolicited private conversations from former trustees, while on duty and on patrol in the village, who've advised that they had a severe disdain and dislike for Officer Joe Segreti and have attempted numerous times to pressure to terminate his career by any means that could reflect his age being a factor. I have been told by Chief Filenko that, "it's not wise to get too close to Joey."

I was sent to partner with Officer Segreti in 2015 (I believe as early as late 2014) in order to display increasing proactivity in order to set a standard model for the now in place point evaluation system, in order to allow a means for Chief Filenko and Deputy Chief Burch to relieve Officer Segreti from duty. I was advised by both Chief Filenko and Deputy Chief Burch that the point determined evaluation system was incepted in order to attempt to end Officer Segreti's career, in that Officer Segreti would not be able to maintain the system.

In a conversation with Commander Lepe and Colon, post their command staff meeting with Chief Filenko, I was advised by both commanders that Chief Filenko expressed outraged at the point system in that Officer Segreti was surpassing the standard, whereas officers like myself were not, having Chief Filenko stated, "What the fuck, how is he scamming the system?"

Appendix I

Prior to becoming the Round Lake Park Police Department MAP Union president, I was non-union and fair share and had numerous private conversations with Chief Filenko, while in his office at 215 E Main St, where I advised in my part a willingness to enter the union in order to obtain an advantage for discipline for Chief Filenko over officers, including Officer Segreti.

I fully acknowledge my part in doing what was requested by Chief Filenko in that he wanted Officer Segreti to be an "easier target" for discipline as Chief Filenko discussed his personal history with Officer Segreti with me, including a friendship which had fallen out and now was at the heading of Chief Filenko no longer wanting Officer Segreti as a part of the Round Lake Park Police Department.

After becoming the MAP union president, Tony Colon and Hector Lepe advised me that during a staff meeting at 215 E Main St, Chief George Filenko stated, "we have our man in the union" and that I would be the officer to aid in removing Officer Segreti.

I submit that my involvement with the special operations, including numerous search warrants, events, patrol operations and more, while during 2013 through 2015 placed me in personal favor with both Chief Filenko and Deputy Chief Dan Burch in that I was privy to personal conversations both in office and on phone, where Chief Filenko made me aware of his intentions towards the progression of officer careers as well as the dismissal of officer careers. I was given preferential treatment for my actions in means of new squad car assignments, overtime approval, special detail allowances, and more.

Chief Filenko and I were in contact with several media outlets, including television production companies, and discussed a future of collaborating on projects, outside of the Round Lake Park Police department. I was in daily contact with Chief Filenko and considered him to be a mentor and confidant and had daily candid "open door" conversations with Chief Filenko while in his office at 215 E Main St. I was told to address Chief Filenko as "George" by himself and we had regular, daily discussions on the progression of the Round Lake Park Police Department, including the unethical practice of Chief Filenko giving me insight history on the past discipline of Commanders Hector Lepe and Tony Colon, including his involvement as well as their limited ability to function as full commanders, due to their limited responsibility. I believe you will recall my outspoken praise for Chief Filenko to yourself while at 2015's national night out. There is further documented proof via facebook posts, both written and video, of my praise for department command staff.

I had a personal and intimate relationship with Chief Filenko in the nature of conversations and discussing other officer's activity, discipline and future. Chief Filenko, while in his office at 215 E Main, discussed his emotional feeling of being "betrayed" by past officers Bonaroti, MaGee and current Officer Segreti in that he believes theirs was of collusion against him by those officers to remove him from his position as Chief of Police.

I believe this to be a violation of GO 3-1 in a supervisory capacity and a violation of ethical behavior.

Consistent Involvement in Ongoing Litigation

Without having detailed information about former Officer Bonaroti's lawsuit or being able to talk about the current federal lawsuit, I respectfully request the village board look

Appendix I

at the claims brought forth in the lawsuit, whereas was involved George Filenko with E Tjarksen.

The complaint provides the following section:

"Case: 1:03-cv-0188

In December 1998, Plaintiff was promoted to shift manager, with eight individuals working under him. (Compl., ¶ 5). During the next three years, Plaintiff received high annual reviews and ratings (averaging 4.5 out of 5.0 system). (Compl., ¶ 6). In the Spring of 1999, Tjarksen observed his immediate supervisor, George Filenko ("Filenko") spending the vast majority of his time on non-Lake County matters. (Compl., ¶ 7).[1] Plaintiff observed Filenko holding meetings, reviewing reports, making conference calls, and having division employees run criminal histories on the computer, all behaviors that Tjarksen believed had nothing to do with Lake County business, but rather, with Filenko's employment

[1] While working for the Lake County Sheriff's Office, Filenko was also employed as Chief of Police in Hainesville, Illinois. (Is something missing here?.......)

with Hainesville. (Compl., ¶ 9). In September 2001, after many months of observing Filenko's activities, Plaintiff reported the conduct to Filenko's direct supervisor, Richard Eckenstahler. (Compl., ¶ 10). Subsequently, Filenko called Tjarksen into his office and questioned Plaintiff about the "double-dipping" report. (Compl., ¶ 11). From that point forward, Plaintiff was subjected to intensive supervision, a restriction in the number of days he could take off, and his file was loaded with reports of trivial and petty infractions. (Compl., ¶ 12). In addition, Tjarksen scored poorly in his annual review, and was transferred to the midnight shift. Id. Ultimately, in July 2002, Tjarksen was terminated from his job at the Lake County Sheriff's Office. (Compl., ¶ 13)."

I respectfully request the village board match the above complaint to the exact timeline I submitted for Tony Colon, Hector Lepe and myself, whereas the discipline distributed under Chief Filenko is identical to his past practice when he is the target of scrutiny or lawsuit.

I further request the village board contact all employees, both civilian and sworn, who have abruptly left the Village of Round Lake Park while under the command of George Filenko and were not allotted an exit interview with the village board.

The above post of "double-dipping" further supports my personal observations in my complaint of Chief Filenko's prioritizing all other projects over the needs of the Round Lake Park Police Department.

I have personally observed Chief Filenko work on all matters non Round Lake Park related, while in his office at 215 E Main St, including county-related matters, post his involvement with Lake County Major Crimes Task Force, his communicating with producers for television segments, book writing deals, Lake County initiatives such as a Way Out and more. George Filenko does not supervise the day to day operations of the Round Lake Park Police Department, however, is merely updated via Deputy Chief Dan Burch, Commander Lepe and daily emailed roll call.

Inability to control anger issues

I have observed Chief Filenko slamming doors, yelling expletive and foul language, talking slanderously about officers and personnel and believe this is a direct correlation to his 2008 ordered anger management, in which he still maintains an inability to control.

Appendix I

Inability to maintain the integrity of legal investigative evidence

It was brought to my attention and then later to my accusation of involvement, of the leaked Round Lake Park Police body camera footage of Hector Lepe and Donna O'Brien to online websites. I submit that this footage was in both the possession of Hector Lepe, Tony Colon and Chief Filenko. The inability to maintain the integrity of the evidence falls under suspicion of Chief Filenko as to date, he has not provided the officers, who are the victims of this offense, where the footage has gone nor whose possession it is in. Furthermore, Chief Filenko's involvement with the footage, on any level, condoned by the mayor and the village, is a direct conflict of interest in the federal lawsuit, unethical and highly suspicious in nature.

Lacking in legitimate and credible police/patrol experience

To date, there is no credible history of Chief Filenko having any direct patrol experience as that of a police officer. The fact that his appointment to the Office of Chief, after being only a dispatcher and administrative commander, shows his inability to properly lead, direct or manage the needs of the Village of Round Lake Park from a community protection and service aspect.

I was advised by Chief Filenko in 2015, that "during my time as Chief, the crime statistics have not changed and gotten worse year by year."

I submit to the village board, that this statement, in itself is a direct admission of Chief Filenko's inability to function at the command level due to his lack of experience.

Drawing consistent negative attention

> I submit to the mayor and the village board to review the involvement of Chief Filenko in both the Melissa Calusinski investigation, the suicide and FBI involvement for the Gliniewicz case and the relationship to Chief Filenko.
>
> I implore the village board to sit and fully review the Calusinski case regardless of the current jury verdict and recognize that an inexperienced Chief Filenko's involvement in her conviction, and future overturning of her conviction, is bringing negative national attention to the village.
>
> His current and consistent involvement in litigation and his loss of nearly twenty (20) officers during his time in command and his part in the dissolving of the Hainesville police department has cast a heavy shadow on the integrity of the village of Round Lake Park and must be considered as fact.

Inability to maintain command structure

> Having been involved as a five (5) year veteran of the Round Lake Beach Police Department, I will submit my professional assessment of the lack of command structure, the makeshift chain of command, the unstructured patrol matrix and the common practice of nepotism and favoritism in the Round Lake Park Police Department.
>
> I submit to the board that there is, to date, convoluted orders issued by Chief George Filenko, on officers to report to different chain of commands while on duty. Although clearly outlined in GO, the matrix has been altered and changed time over by Chief Filenko to continually maintain a sense of segregation between both day and night shift, as well as the detective office and command staff.

Appendix I

There is no structured "OIC" (Officer in Charge) while on shift, as Officer Reuter is the only certified OIC the department has.

Furthermore, Deputy Chief Dan Burch sent out an order not to contact Commander Lepe during his off time, yet there is no access to command, including Deputy Chief Burch either delaying or not answering phone calls or emails for officers when times of command is required. Furthermore, when advised to contact Commander Lepe via Deputy Chief Burch, he does not answer nor return calls, which can be observed in a recent potential child abduction case at 108 E Willow.

I also submit to the village board and inquiry as to why Officer Joey Segreti and Officer Randy Reuter are partners on one midnight shift, having a nearly combined sixty (60) years of law enforcement experience, while Officer Donna O'Brien and Officer Valle have less than a total combined year of full-time experience between them both on a midnight shift where they go most times without supervision.

I submit that Officer Valle was not properly or completely trained, as he was removed from FTO officers Colon and myself and Officer Donna O'Brien was commented on not having the qualifications to serve another department if she left Round Lake Park.

I respectfully request the board look into why Officer O'Brien was hired over all other candidates on the list she was a part of, if in fact, according to a statement by Deputy Chief Burch that she was unqualified.

I submit this is a direct correlation to an inappropriate and unprofessional personal relationship between Officer

O'Brien and Deputy Chief Dan Burch as she confided in with Tony Colon while she was on FTO with him.

I have made Chief Filenko aware, via written memo, of numerous and ongoing policy and command violations from Officer O'Brien, with no action taken to correct her behavior. This is due to nepotism and is a risk to both Officer O'Brien's safety, other officer's safety and every member of the village of Round Lake Park in which she served.

I have been accused of singling out and attacking Officer O'Brien, however, will stand by the statement that nearly all of the officers of the Round Lake Park Police Department, as well as bordering agencies, do not support her employment as a police officer in that her tactics and judgment are undertrained and uneducated. I have repeatedly asked for training and correction for her improved ability from Commander Lepe and Colon, both who stated they will not relay any such request for training for fear of retaliation of Deputy Chief Dan Burch as they all are aware of his close and personal relationship with Officer O'Brien.

The most recent and direct example of her inability to properly serve is in the unethical and potential illegal arrest of Brian Johnson of 411 Elder.

I urge the village board to inquire as to why Johnson, a known resident with a mental handicap, who makes nearly daily and nightly contact with every officer in the village, was arrested on village ordinance for Public Intoxication, handcuffed and escorted home.

This issue and great concern was brought to the attention to Commander Lepe, with supporting past practice evidence of its illegal nature, as prohibited by Illinois State Law, as

Appendix I

well as the unethical practice of arresting a mentally handicapped man who's brother and mother had recently died, who is furthermore unable to pay the fine of $250.

Commander Lepe returned my inquiry with a personal conversation of threats for discipline if I further requested Officer O'Brien be educated properly to ensure she be able to serve. I submit to the village board the investigation of the common practice of arresting for village ordinance for Public Intoxication and the potential issue of officers conducting illegal arrests, violating our resident's civil rights.

This is also a common practice for Chief Filenko to not consider the expertise of his command staff and training personnel, as can been seen in the documentation and notification of Commander Colon, Commander Lepe, Deputy Chief Dan Burch and myself and the concerns and inability to perform his duty to expectation by Officer Walter Rodriguez.

Chief Filenko's failure to take counsel of the information on Officer Rodriguez has attributed to the witnessed unethical and potential illegal practice that officers have observed Officer Rodriguez enter into vehicles he stops, based on probable cause that other officers to not concur with.

Furthermore, the recent hiring of Robert Cavaiani is continued notice of nepotism and preferential treatment as his close and historical friendship with Chief Filenko has clouded Filenko's judgment on discipline.

In a recently shared call to the Round Lake Senior Highschool, I responded to the call and was issued a letter of reprimand on three (3) counts which I submitted to your office.

Officer Cavaiani responded to the same call, as a probationary officer, with a juvenile detainee in the rear of his squad car and was issued a letter of contact. This is clear and intentional preferential treatment for Chief Filenko's friend, who was hired after he quit the Gurnee police department, abruptly.

I submit that the village board investigate these instances.

The division created by Chief George Filenko is historically documented by former personnel and can be seen, in action, on a daily occurrence. It is furthered with the command staff, including Commander Lepe and Deputy Chief Burch, both who have confided in me their disapproval for Filenko's leadership, tactics, command ability and future with the Round Lake Park Police Department. Commander Lepe has confided in me that due to his age and fear of his inability to secure outside employment, he has submitted to Chief Filenko's unethical and immoral command practices. Deputy Chief Burch has confided in me that due to his closing in on his twentieth year of service and family to support, he "gave up " a long time ago.

I have received numerous emails, calls and in-person contacts from former personnel, who all advised the same tactics used by Chief Filenko to achieve dissension and chaotic behavior within the department, with Chief Filenko maintaining a disassociation as to remain un-implacable.

Mayor and Trustees, you have a severe and cancerous problem within the police department.

I have done my part to contribute to the solution of the problem and now have fallen victim to the highly suspect behavior of Chief Filenko who commonly eradicates all challenges to his integrity via discipline and termination.

I submit that due to fear of retaliation from Chief Filenko, I will receive little to no support in my claims from other officers. I will, however, be sending you supporting documents of all my claims for your review, which have also been submitted to my attorney.

I urge you all to look into the matter, investigate fully and resolve the issue as your families and selves are residents of the village of Round Lake Park and deserve the epitome of public service…of which you are far lacking while Chief Filenko holds his title.

It is my wish to continue service to the village and assist in restoring the public trust and department integrity and urge the village board and mayor support my doing so.

Respectfully,
Officer Dominick Izzo #501

APPENDIX II

My Open Response to Backstabbing the Blue:
George, I want to reply to your recent article in Law Enforcement Today titled Backstabbing the Blue.

You do realize that you used the death of a police officer to justify your bad hiring practices, right? George, re-read your article it wasn't about Officer Corona, it was about you, yet again, like everything is.

You see, George, you validate my point.

Sad as it is that Officer Corona lost her life, it wasn't about her age that cost her life. Her age put her in a position to be hired and placed in harm's way to have her lose it.

Perhaps she would still be alive today if there was an increase in the age policy that prevented her to be hired, but we can go back and forth all day and argue that point.

I don't expect you to understand this, because you never served the public, you weren't ever a cop.

You wore the uniform as a part-time police officer in your late 40's and went straight to appointed administrative roles out of a favor from the corrupt political ties that you wrote about. You didn't think people were going to stay silent forever, did you?

There are no "routine calls" as you pointed out in your article. Had you worked the street, you'd have known that.

I am willing to bet my experience as a police officer, which as a street cop far exceeds yours, that Officer Corona's killer took her life for only one reason, and that's because he felt he could.

Sadly, age and its perception do play a very large role in a suspect's actions against an officer. And if the man was alive today, I am certain he would have validated my views, as horrible as they are.

You see George, I'm not targeting your new officers, I'm targeting your decision to hire them.

Over the years, you've hired officers who are impressionable and can be controlled. I believe you recently told someone that, "Izzo will never be reinstated because I can't control him." You're damn right, you can't.

But a woman with gang ties and three baby faced officers who can't even wear their uniforms properly for their graduation can be controlled, considering they would most likely not get hired by any other agencies.

But I'm sure, like the dozens before them, they will spend a year at your agency and leave to another after gaining experience and seeing right through you as we all did.

Did you include your hiring practices and retention rate in your article?

Does the publisher know you've lost nearly 30 police officers to other agencies while your time as a police chief in a 10 officer department?

Does the publisher and the reader know that as chief, you've been sued several times including for harassment, had your evidence room broken into, lost narcotics, been ordered by your village board to anger management, been accused of mishandling crucial evidence, have been criticized for mishandling several murder cases and even violate your own department policies over and over? Does anyone else know about your iPhone that's filled with pictures of crime scene dead bodies that you show people in public?

George, stop kidding yourself. You fired only one officer in your career as chief after he didn't accept your offer to resign and he demanded your resignation.

As for the "too many reasons to list" you say he was fired for, why not mention his name in your article and show all of his catastrophic and grievous unbecoming conduct?

C'mon, the public should see all those "Facebook posts of pictures in uniform" he was fired for. Pretty serious stuff George.

Appendix II

No worries, I wouldn't give me any more free press either. After all, it was all the press and media coverage I was getting that made you so jealous that you just had to fire me... for a text message.

I doubt you'd write about the federal lawsuit I filed against you and the suspected criminal conduct you were allegedly engaged in that really were the reasons you got rid of me.

Please, continue about my indiscretions in law enforcement and don't write about your own. Wasn't it a Las Vegas scandal and abuse of county funds that forced you to resign from your job as a dispatcher director? What was that issue with county that got you in a lawsuit? Wasn't it "double-dipping" and collecting two paychecks funded by taxpayers while only working one job? I don't recall, maybe you can write about it in your next article.

While you're at it, I can't recall, George, what was the reason you were fired from Hainesville Police Department? And what was it that the mayor said when asked if they would ever allow you to supervise police on their streets again?

Losing that contract and the public trust must have been upsetting. But feel free to discuss other officers and keep thinking your title as chief gives you validation.

Chickens always come home to roost.

You have pure contempt for police officers. You always have and I don't blame you. Jealousy comes from a place of extreme inner pain and conflict.

Your own command sees this. You should ask me how many times your Deputy Chief, a real cop and Marine, and I would have coffee and I'd watch the eyes roll in his head while we discussed your inept ability to run a department.

Do I have to remind you of your recent condescending posting on a Lake County "Street Deputy" who I've personally worked alongside?

Did you mention in your post how the officer has gained national attention as a television personality and you can't stand that? That street deputy has done more in his time as a cop for his community than you could ever come close to. I know, I was there with him on calls where he saved my ass a time or two and I'd follow him through hell for it.

We would have you wait outside the gates, so you didn't get lost along the way.

I guess no one needs to know about your incessant need to talk to a camera and any officer who challenges you in that realm gains your Filenko fury quite quickly.

You never were a cop, George. You don't get it and never will.

See, you put 4 kids on the street and placed their lives in danger. They are a part of a generation who are not ready to serve the public. But they are ready to be controlled by you and that's why police officers today are under fire. They don't know any better.

They look to guidance from men in positions of power like you, but they are really being moved as pawns for your own personal game.

I can almost visualize each of them being ordered back to Post 6 just to have to sit in your office and listen to your boring stories over and over and your false promises of positions in the department that don't even exist. Another daily hell I had to go through.

Smile and nod, smile and nod. Let him talk so you can just get back on the road.

As sad and tragic as it is, Officer Corona's loss of life isn't the issue as your article points out. You couldn't have missed a bigger target if you were blindfolded and spun the opposite direction.

Officer Corona was part of a tragically small percentage of cops who still have to do a job, day in and day out while serving the public.

That's what you missed. It's not about her life. It's about the countless lives out there still serving those who need and depend on them.

The public, George, the public. They are what matters, but you wouldn't know that, you never worked with them.

You never did. You don't get it. You were a call taker who was seated behind a desk (and you disgrace dispatchers) and a "yes man" to someone who had corrupt political pull and gave you a task force that was so successful at false convictions that even the governor wanted it shut down.

All officers face death daily. And all officers face serving daily. But you glanced right over that because you saw an opportunity to use a forum to validate your severely misguided judgment in hiring. And the residents of your town are well aware of it.

No academy, no scrutinized Illinois hiring practice and no independent police review board who is in their late 70's and 80's and friends of the mayor will ever replace life experience and the human empathy necessary to become a real police officer.

Sadly, once again, the position of chief is appointed and not earned. And we both know who got you your gold badge.

George, trust me, all 4 of your officers together couldn't secure me into custody. And that's not a challenge, that's a scary statement of an inability to serve those who someday may need protection from someone much tougher than me.

And considering that we both know that you would hide behind all of them if ever challenged by me face to face again. And if I were you, based on who you hired, I'd probably wet my pants.

Retire George, you've ruined law enforcement pretending to be something just so you could have a take-home car and people who were forced to listen to your stories, considering everyone at home tuned you out years ago.

Respectfully,
Dominick Izzo
Ex-Police Officer, but was a real one none the less.